The
Reference Shelf ®

U.S. National Debate Topic 2010–2011

The American Military Presence Overseas

Edited by Kenneth Partridge

The Reference Shelf
Volume 82 • Number 3
The H.W. Wilson Company
New York • Dublin
2010

The Reference Shelf

The books in this series contain reprints of articles, excerpts from books, addresses on current issues, and studies of social trends in the United States and other countries. There are six separately bound numbers in each volume, all of which are usually published in the same calendar year. Numbers one through five are each devoted to a single subject, providing background information and discussion from various points of view and concluding with a subject index and comprehensive bibliography that lists books, pamphlets, and abstracts of additional articles on the subject. The final number of each volume is a collection of recent speeches, and it contains a cumulative speaker index. Books in the series may be purchased individually or on subscription.

Library of Congress has cataloged this serial title as follows:

U.S. national debate topic, 2010–2011 : the American military presence overseas / edited by Kenneth Partridge.
   p. cm. — (The reference shelf ; v. 82, no. 3)
   Includes bibliographical references.
   ISBN 978-0-8242-1098-4 (alk. paper)
1. United States—Armed Forces--Foreign countries. 2. United States—Military relations—Foreign countries. 3. Military bases, American—Foreign countries. 4. United States—Military policy. I. Partridge, Kenneth, 1980- II. Title: American military presence overseas.
   UA26.A2U25 2010
   355'.0310973—dc22

                          2010015321

Cover: U.S. Soldiers with Blackwatch Company, 2nd Battalion, 1st Infantry Regiment speak with village elders at a Kuchi village in Hutal, Afghanistan, March 17, 2010. (U.S. Air Force photo by Staff Sgt. Dayton Mitchell/Released)

Visit H.W. Wilson's Web site: www.hwwilson.com

Printed in the United States of America

Contents

Preface

The 1991 fall of the Soviet Union marked a symbolic end to the "American Century," a period in which the United States surpassed the Old World European powers and achieved global dominance. Having turned the tide in two world wars and outlasted Russia's "Evil Empire," to quote President Ronald Reagan, the United States stood as the last remaining superpower, a hegemonic juggernaut with unmatched political, economic, and cultural influence.

The triumph followed nearly 50 years of Cold War military build-up, and if, in the wake of the Soviet collapse, the United States suddenly found itself lacking real rivals, it remained well equipped to handle any that might arise. U.S. overseas military bases numbered in the hundreds, dotting the globe from the South Pacific to the Arctic, and after the terror attacks of September 11, 2001, the United States further extended its reach, brokering "gas and go" deals with African, Asian, and South American nations willing to aid in its War on Terror.

By 2009, the U.S. military had come to control an estimated 795,000 acres of land—territory enough to house some 190,000 troops on more than 1,000 bases in dozens of countries.

Much of this military might was—and, as of this writing, is—concentrated in Afghanistan and Iraq, nations the United States and its allies invaded in 2001 and 2003, respectively. The latter campaign, though not strictly speaking a unilateral action, proved wildly controversial, igniting international debate over whether the United States has the right to launch preemptive strikes against countries accused of supporting terrorists. Such longtime European allies as Germany and France criticized the effort, and President George W. Bush became a divisive figure, symbolizing, for better or worse, the United States' willingness and ability to topple regimes deemed threats to security.

While Bush's successor, Barack Obama, announced in 2009 exit strategies for both Iraq and Afghanistan, questions concerning how and when the United States should flex its military muscle remain unanswered. Mindful of this point, the National Forensics League chose as its 2010–2011 debate topic the following: "Resolved: The United States federal government should substantially reduce its military and/or police presence in one or more of the following: South Korea, Japan, Afghanistan, Kuwait, Iraq, Turkey." This edition of the Reference Shelf is intended as a starting point for students tasked with debating this complex topic, and the articles collected herein focus on U.S. relations with five countries: Afghanistan, Iraq, Turkey, Japan, and South Korea.

Selections in the first chapter, "Rome Revisited? The U.S. Military Presence Around the World," provide an overview of global U.S. troop deployments and consider whether the country has become an empire, as many critics contend. While it hasn't set up formal colonies, as the British and Romans once did, the United States nevertheless flies its flag over military installations in all corners of the world. It also wields unparalleled economic influence, selling McDonalds hamburgers and Starbucks lattes, to name but two ubiquitous products, wherever markets exist. In his piece "Too Many Overseas Bases," David Vine avoids the question of imperialism and argues America's offshore bases are simply too costly, both in terms of dollars and damage to the country's reputation, to maintain. Thomas Donnelly, meanwhile, offers "Two Cheers for the US Empire!" lauding the nation's stabilizing presence around the globe.

Pieces in the next chapter, "Afghanistan: 'Graveyard of Empires'?" center on the first major battleground in the U.S. War on Terror, a desolate Asian nation whose ousted Taliban government once harbored 9/11 mastermind Osama bin Laden and his al-Qaeda conspirators. Many of the selections focus on President Barack Obama's 2009 decision to implement a troop "surge" followed by a withdrawal of forces 18 months later. Some critics have labeled the surge too little, too late, while others view the entire Afghanistan operation as wrongheaded, since al-Qaeda militants—bin Laden included—have likely fled the country.

The third chapter, "Iraq: Should We Stay or Should We Go?" contains selections that examine the feasibility and wisdom of Obama's plan to withdraw all American forces by 2011. Even as relatively peaceful national elections held in March 2010 spurred hopes for a stable, self-sufficient Iraq—something that might have seemed unthinkable during the war's bloody early years—U.S. military officials began discussing the possibility of extending the deadline and providing further assistance to the country's young government and unproven security forces.

Articles in the fourth section, "Turkey: Strategic Crossroads," highlight the United States' increasingly complex relationship with a country that straddles both a literal and figurative divide between the West and the Middle East. Traditionally a staunch U.S. ally, Turkey has, in recent years, instituted a "zero problems with neighbors" policy—one that has prevented it from supporting the invasion of Iraq and a hard-line stance against Iran, much to Washington's chagrin.

Entries in the fifth and six chapters examine the United States' longstanding military alliances with Japan and South Korea, respectively. Whereas both partnerships made sense 50 years ago, at the dawn of the Cold War, the new century has brought new challenges. Despite the threat of North Korean nuclear armament, northeast Asia no longer carries the strategic importance it once did, and wars of the future will likely not be fought by large contingents of ground soldiers. What's more, a growing number of Japanese and South Korean citizens are calling for a withdrawal of U.S. forces, citing as reasons the pollution, criminal activity, and noise disturbances that tend to accompany bases. Both nations may also want to distance themselves from U.S. policies that could lead to problems with their Asian neighbors.

In conclusion, I would like to express my sincerest gratitude to the many authors and publishers who allowed us to reprint the articles used in this book. I must also thank my wife, Lindsey, who's always game for a good political discussion, as well as my H.W. Wilson coworkers Paul McCaffrey and Richard Stein, talented, hard-working editors who, given a couple of hours, a few pots of coffee, and a copy of the board game Risk, just might solve this global-military conundrum once and for all.

Kenneth Partridge
June 2010

1

Rome Revisited?
The U.S. Military Presence Around the World

Editor's Introduction

Taking into account Iraq and Afghanistan—active war zones, as of this writing—the U.S. military maintains more than 1,000 overseas bases. Some, like the Ramstein Air Base in Germany, are home to thousands of servicemen and women, as well as their families. These large-scale bases, dubbed "little Americas," often contain schools, fast-food restaurants, shopping centers, and even golf courses. Others are smaller and less permanent. So-called "cooperative security locations," or "lily pads," for example, are bare-bones facilities with limited full-time personnel. These installations are designed to become operational as needed, enabling U.S. forces to fly in, set up shop, and quickly respond to conflicts whenever and wherever they arise.

The United States began amassing its global network of military bases in the aftermath of World War II. Between 1938 and 1948, the number of foreign installations jumped from 14 to 30,000. Throughout the Cold War, the U.S. military used as justification for this expansion the threat of communist aggression. While the much-feared showdown with the Soviets never came to pass, the United States waged bloody wars against communism in such locations as Korea and Vietnam, demonstrating its willingness to intervene in foreign affairs. Whether such campaigns were well-intentioned or rooted in American self-interest remains a matter of debate.

A decade after the fall of the Soviet Union, the terror attacks of September 11, 2001, pitted the United States against a new enemy, an informal cabal of Islamic extremists operating without the support of a specific state. The administration of President George W. Bush responded by launching the War on Terror, a borderless, open-ended campaign to thwart Jihadist fighters and prevent future attacks. By 2003 the United States had invaded two countries, Afghanistan and Iraq, and launched covert operations in many others.

The articles in this chapter provide an overview of the global U.S. military presence and present arguments for and against foreign troop deployments. In his editorial "Diplomacy Gone Astray," the first piece, Edward Cuddy draws parallels between the United States and the Roman Empire. It's a common comparison, one that has been the subject of numerous books and articles, and in making his case for more diplomacy and less military intervention, Cuddy cautions that the United States has, like Rome before it, overextended its military and initiated wars it can't afford. Warning that unwise use of power could lead to America's self-destruction, he quotes the British historian Arnold J. Toynbee: "Civilizations die from suicide, not by murder."

In the second selection, "Too Many Overseas Bases," David Vine decries the high cost—measured both in dollars and damage to America's reputation—of maintaining troop presence in other countries. Vine claims that bases breed anti-American sentiment and heighten tensions in troubled regions. Catherine Lutz makes similar points in "Obama's Empire," the next piece, debunking the idea that American bases benefit host nations. "The immediate negative effects include levels of pollution, noise, crime, and lost productive land that cannot be offset by soldiers local spending or employment of local people," she writes. Lutz also cites examples of the United States displacing populations and supporting crooked regimes in order to gain land for bases.

"Two Cheers for the US Empire!" the subsequent entry in this chapter, finds Thomas Donnelly taking a more favorable view of America's military prowess. "What is historically distinct about U.S. power is that it correlates quite remarkably with the spread of human liberty and representative government, through time and across cultures," he writes, insisting the United States promotes peace and stability.

In the next selection, "The American Non-Empire," Ed Morrissey agrees with *Los Angeles Times* writer Jonah Goldberg's assertion that the United States ought not to be labeled an "empire," but rather "leader of the free world." Goldberg argues that overseas U.S. military bases are nothing like British or Roman colonies, and he dismisses the idea that the ubiquity of American popular culture is somehow the result of coercion. The U.S. military promotes "free trade," Morrissey writes, but it "doesn't impose 'Seinfield' on foreigners any more than China imposes T-shirts on Americans."

In the final article, "Obama to Confront Limits of America's Overstretched Military," Anna Mulrine discusses the nation's growing demand for more troops. According to several military officials, the current force falls short of what is needed to carry out missions in Iraq, Afghanistan, and elsewhere. In response, recruiters have lowered their educational requirements and increased "sign-up bonuses," offering some would-be soldiers as much as $40,000.

Diplomacy Gone Astray[*]

Obama Is in Eye of the Storm in Volatile Middle East

By Edward Cuddy
Buffalo News, January 24, 2010

In the late 18th century, Edward Gibbon published his enduring classic, "The Decline and Fall of the Roman Empire." Rome's demise, he explained, "was the inevitable effect of immoderate greatness. Prosperity ripened the principle of decay; the causes of destruction multiplied with the extent of conquest . . . [eventually] the stupendous fabric yielded to the pressure of its own weight."

Today, the United States is edging toward a similar stage of "imperial over-stretch," as historian Paul Kennedy described it—a great power in relative decline, diverting resources from productive economic investment to unproductive wars and armaments while competitor nations devote more of their wealth to "productive investments for long-term growth."

America, once the greatest creditor in the world, has become the world's greatest debtor—a spendthrift nation spending beyond its means to maintain worldwide military dominance and an extravagant lifestyle, increasingly beholden to foreign creditors.

Our fate, however, is not preordained. Adversity is the engine of progress, as historian Arnold Toynbee concluded in his "Study of History," tracing the rise and fall of world civilizations. Societies progress by responding to "challenges of special difficulty," he claimed, "which spurs [people] to make hitherto unprecedented efforts" to survive.

But great powers can hit bottom when challenges are overwhelming or leaders lack the wisdom or moral strength to manage them.

Consider foreign relations—specifically, three hot spots in the volatile Middle East: Afghanistan, Israel and Iran. Assume that our "imperial overstretch" is central to America's struggle to survive and thrive in our global village.

At the eye of the storm is President Obama, who sailed to victory in 2008, projecting a persona graced with the qualities to master the nation's daunting challenges. In several addresses, Obama engaged people worldwide with a cosmopolitan diplomacy, shorn of his predecessor's unilateralism, calling for a new era of cooperation to solve global problems.

In his Cairo address on June 4, Obama spoke of America's own aggression in the Middle East, reaching out to people who had felt the sting of American power in many forms ranging from overthrowing governments to economic sanctions and military assaults.

By the 1990s, the Arab-Muslim world had become fertile soil for Osama bin Laden's terrorist campaign, culminating in the 9/11 attacks against the World Trade Center and the Pentagon, the symbols of American military and economic power. In response, President George W. Bush conquered and occupied Afghanistan and Iraq, which, in turn, engulfed occupiers and occupied in a cauldron of violence and terrorism.

In contrast to Iraq, Afghanistan was the "good war," targeting bin Laden's command center harbored under Kabul's Taliban regime. But a war launched against his al-Qaida outsiders has morphed into a Vietnam-type struggle against Afghan Taliban militants with a long history of expelling foreign invaders. Today, we are fighting on a terrain favoring suicide bombers and guerrilla ambushes, relying on a corrupt and unpopular government in Kabul, chasing elusive al-Qaida militants mostly outside of Afghanistan—and, arguably, fighting the wrong enemy. Obama's exit strategy, beefing up American forces to strengthen Afghans to stand on their own, may be ignoring the most effective outlet from the struggle: "to make friends among enemies," as MIT analyst Michael Semple argues.

Our best bet is a "political surge," exploiting the strains within the Taliban/al-Qaida alliance and leading to a settlement based on the withdrawal of U.S. forces and a Taliban commitment to neutralize or eject al-Qaida. Military force, carefully calibrated to hold the line while negotiating a truce with Taliban leaders, may be necessary. But a campaign to bust the enemy could sink America into the bloody quicksands of Afghanistan as the Russians did in the 1980s, hastening the collapse of the Soviet Union.

In the thorny struggle against terrorism, where friends and foes mix together, Obama has adopted two significant strategies: drain the swamp of anti-Americanism by addressing the legitimate grievances of the Arab-Muslim world and enlist allies to help with the Herculean struggle to stabilize the region.

It's a formula tailor-made for the Israeli-Palestinian conflict, a major source of the region's anti-Americanism. Indeed, Obama did demand a freeze on Israeli settlements en route to a Palestinian state, a clue signaling Washington's new role as an impartial peacemaker. Stick to his guns, and Obama can siphon the air out of Hamas and Hezbollah, while undercutting bin Laden's self-serving justifications for 9/11.

The Arab League, including 22 countries, was already on the same page, allies in waiting since 2002 for an American president to weigh in as an honest broker. Fearful of the anti-American and anti-Israeli hatreds agitating the region, Saudi King Abdullah had persuaded the league to promise permanent peace for Israel in return for its withdrawal from the occupied territory and acceptance of a Palestinian state.

Obama himself praised Abdullah's blueprint, raising hopes for an all-out surge toward the two-state solution. Unfortunately, Israeli Prime Minister Benjamin Netanyahu, longtime opponent of Palestinian sovereignty, continued the old game, settling more Israelis in the West Bank and East Jerusalem while piously calling for renewed peace negotiations. In response, Obama merely issued a juiceless objection, forfeiting some of the good will he had cultivated in the Islamic world.

Having brushed aside his Arab would-be allies, Obama has compromised America's war against al-Qaida terrorism further by turning Iran, a potential ally, into an enemy. Lost in the current polemics over Iran's nuclear ambitions are the vital security interests linking the two countries. Both nations oppose al-Qaida; both fear the prospect of Pakistan's nuclear weapons falling into terrorists' hands. When Bush overthrew Saddam Hussein's Sunni regime, Iran's worst regional enemy, Tehran promptly recognized the American-backed Shiite regime. Iran's soldiers supported America's war against the Taliban/al-Qaida forces in Afghanistan. And when Bush recklessly diverted American forces from Afghanistan to Iraq, Iranians stayed the course, investing $560 million to modernize Afghanistan's scratch-scrabble economy.

Instead of welcoming Iran as an ally, Bush blacklisted it on his "axis-of-evil" list, reviving bitter memories dating back to 1953 when the CIA overthrew Iran's democratic government, wreaking havoc on the Iranian people for decades. For good reason, Obama insisted on negotiations with Tehran last October, despite heated criticism. The first president to admit Washington's aggression in the 1953 coup, Obama has expressed hopes for Iran's support in Afghanistan and Iraq. During his campaign for a nuclear-free world, he acknowledged his awkward situation—forbidding Iran to "pursue their nuclear weapons" while maintaining "our own stockpiles."

Nevertheless, since the negotiations failed to dissolve suspicions regarding Iran's nuclear plans, Obama has been mobilizing other countries to tighten economic sanctions on Iran—a position that drew criticism from several analysts. Consider some of their points: Washington must address Iran's security concerns—surrounded by three nuclear powers, under direct threats from the United States and Israel and the possibility of Pakistan's nuclear arsenal falling into terrorists' hands; deal with the nuclear question through Obama's campaign for a nuclear-free world; and enlist Iran into a coalition with China, Russia and India to help stabilize the region and to reinforce Pakistan's struggle to keep her nuclear weapons from falling into al-Qaida and Taliban militants.

"The enemy of my enemy is my friend," says an Arab proverb. During World War II, President Franklin D. Roosevelt joined forces with Stalin's brutal Soviet regime to conquer Nazi Germany. While pursuing his 1972 detente policy, President Richard M. Nixon engaged Communist China, bristling with nuclear weapons, to contain Soviet expansionism. Bush's "surge" in Iraq succeeded (partly) by recruiting Sunni terrorists to fight al-Qaida terrorists. Why not Iran against al-Qaida?

In the long run, America's revival depends less on our wealth and power than on the wisdom to use them: in times of conflict, the wisdom to define objectives that truly serve the nation's interests; a strong preference for diplomacy over force; and an understanding of the limits, even the boomerang effect of military force.

"Civilizations die from suicide, not by murder," Toynbee concluded after studying the rise and fall of 22 civilizations. The idea of self-destruction was central to bin Laden's devious strategy behind the 9/11 attacks, according to Bruce Riedel, a Middle East expert and adviser to three presidents, including Obama: to "provoke and bait" the United States into "bleeding wars" throughout the Islamic world, in order to bankrupt America as done to the Soviet Union in Afghanistan. Bush, hell-bent to "kick some ass," as an adviser recalled, swallowed the bait, sending American forces into Afghanistan, launching another war with Iraq and alienating Iran. Now, the conflagration is spreading into Pakistan.

The wars in Iraq and Afghanistan have reached the trillion-dollar mark and rising, not to mention the enormous toll on lives. America's battered economy, the bedrock of our power, is threatened further by bloated military budgets, consuming resources that could put millions of Americans to work rebuilding our crumbling infrastructure, streamlining transit systems, developing green industries, etc. Worse yet is our antitax, free-lunch mentality—the delusion that we can wage wars and maintain living standards on borrowed dollars, surrendering our fate largely to foreign creditors like China and Japan, sliding toward that "debt explosion" that doomed the European empires the past four centuries.

In Toynbee's perspective, America's basic challenge is to check the "suicidal" impulses in our collective behavior and redirect our energies toward upholding the common good against special interests—a daunting task that Obama has addressed in many speeches. His performance, however, has fallen far short of his rhetoric.

The heavy criticism may be premature, considering the complexity of the problems he inherited, the fierce opposition he faced at every turn, and the progress, however modest, he has made. Obama has emerged as a world leader prodding the world community to tackle tough problems from global warming and depression to terrorism and the nuclear "Sword of Damocles" dangling over all of us.

Moreover, the president's voice has widened our political discourse, legitimizing self-criticism when America has wronged other nations and criticizing allies when they endanger American security—the kind of critical analysis seldom heard, but fundamental for realist diplomacy.

Too Many Overseas Bases[*]

By David Vine
Foreign Policy in Focus, February 25, 2009

In the midst of an economic crisis that's getting scarier by the day, it's time to ask whether the nation can really afford some 1,000 military bases overseas. For those unfamiliar with the issue, you read that number correctly. One thousand. One thousand U.S. military bases outside the 50 states and Washington, DC, representing the largest collection of bases in world history.

Officially the Pentagon counts 865 base sites, but this notoriously unreliable number omits all our bases in Iraq (likely over 100) and Afghanistan (80 and counting), among many other well-known and secretive bases. More than half a century after World War II and the Korean War, we still have 268 bases in Germany, 124 in Japan, and 87 in South Korea. Others are scattered around the globe in places like Aruba and Australia, Bulgaria and Bahrain, Colombia and Greece, Djibouti, Egypt, Kuwait, Qatar, Romania, Singapore, and of course, Guantánamo Bay, Cuba—just to name a few. Among the installations considered critical to our national security are a ski center in the Bavarian Alps, resorts in Seoul and Tokyo, and 234 golf courses the Pentagon runs worldwide.

Unlike domestic bases, which set off local alarms when threatened by closure, our collection of overseas bases is particularly galling because almost all our taxpayer money leaves the United States (much goes to enriching private base contractors like corruption-plagued former Halliburton subsidiary KBR). One part of the massive Ramstein airbase near Landstuhl, Germany, has an estimated value of $3.3 billion. Just think how local communities could use that kind of money to make investments in schools, hospitals, jobs, and infrastructure.

Even the Bush administration saw the wastefulness of our overseas basing network. In 2004, then-Secretary of Defense Donald Rumsfeld announced plans to close more than one-third of the nation's overseas installations, moving 70,000 troops and 100,000 family members and civilians back to the United States. National Security Adviser Jim Jones, then commander of U.S. forces in Europe, called for closing 20% of our bases in Europe. According to Rumsfeld's estimates, we could save at least $12 billion by closing 200 to 300 bases alone. While the closures were derailed by claims that closing bases could cost us in the short term, even if this is true, it's no reason to continue our profligate ways in the longer term.

COSTS FAR EXCEEDING DOLLARS AND CENTS

Unfortunately, the financial costs of our overseas bases are only part of the problem. Other costs to people at home and abroad are just as devastating. Military families suffer painful dislocations as troops stationed overseas separate from loved ones or uproot their families through frequent moves around the world. While some foreign governments like U.S. bases for their perceived economic benefits, many locals living near the bases suffer environmental and health damage from military toxins and pollution, disrupted economic, social, and cultural systems, military accidents, and increased prostitution and crime.

In undemocratic nations like Uzbekistan, Kyrgyzstan, and Saudi Arabia, our bases support governments responsible for repression and human rights abuses. In too many recurring cases, soldiers have raped, assaulted, or killed locals, most prominently of late in South Korea, Okinawa, and Italy. The forced expulsion of the entire Chagossian people to create our secretive base on British Diego Garcia in the Indian Ocean is another extreme but not so aberrant example.

Bases abroad have become a major and unacknowledged "face" of the United States, frequently damaging the nation's reputation, engendering grievances and anger, and generally creating antagonistic rather than cooperative relationships between the United States and others. Most dangerously, as we have seen in Saudi Arabia and Yemen, and as we are seeing in Iraq and Afghanistan, foreign bases create breeding grounds for radicalism, anti-Americanism, and attacks on the United States, reducing, rather than improving, our national security.

Proponents of maintaining the overseas base status quo will argue, however, that our foreign bases are critical to national and global security. A closer examination shows that overseas bases have often heightened military tensions and discouraged diplomatic solutions to international conflicts. Rather than stabilizing dangerous regions, our overseas bases have often increased global militarization, enlarging security threats faced by other nations who respond by boosting military spending (and in cases like China and Russia, foreign base acquisition) in an escalating spiral. Overseas bases actually make war more likely, not less.

THE BENEFITS OF FEWER BASES

This isn't a call for isolationism or a protectionism that would prevent us from spending money overseas. As the Obama administration and others have recognized, we must recommit to cooperative forms of engagement with the rest of the world that rely on diplomatic, economic, and cultural ties rather than military means. In addition to freeing money to meet critical human needs at home and abroad, fewer overseas bases would help rebuild our military into a less overstretched, defensive force committed to defending the nation's territory from attack.

In these difficult economic times, the Obama administration and Congress should initiate a major reassessment of our 1,000 overseas bases. Now is the time to ask if, as a nation and a world, we can really afford the 1,000 bases that are pushing the nation deeper into debt and making the United States and the planet less secure? With so many needs facing our nation, it's unconscionable to have 1,000 overseas bases. It's time to begin closing them.

Obama's Empire[*]

By Catherine Lutz
New Statesman, August 3, 2009

In December 2008, shortly before being sworn in as the 44th president of the United States, Barack Obama pledged his belief that, "to ensure prosperity here at home and peace abroad", it was vital to maintain "the strongest military on the planet." Unveiling his national security team, including George Bush's defence secretary, Robert Gates, he said: "We also agree the strength of our military has to be combined with the wisdom and force of diplomacy, and that we are going to be committed to rebuilding and re-strengthening alliances around the world to advance American interests and American security."

Unfortunately, many of the Obama administration's diplomatic efforts are being directed towards maintaining and garnering new access for the US military across the globe. US military officials, through their Korean proxies, have completed the eviction of resistant rice farmers from their land around Camp Humphreys, South Korea, for its expansion (including a new 18-hole golf course); they are busily making back-room deals with officials in the Northern Mariana Islands to gain the use of the Pacific islands there for bombing and training purposes; and they are scrambling to express support for a regime in Kyrgyzstan that has been implicated in the murder of its political opponents but whose Manas Airbase, used to stage US military actions in Afghanistan since 2001, Obama and the Pentagon consider crucial for the expanded war there.

The global reach of the US military today is unprecedented and unparalleled. Officially, more than 190,000 troops and 115,000 civilian employees are massed in approximately 900 military facilities in 46 countries and territories (the unofficial figure is far greater). The US military owns or rents 795,000 acres of land, with 26,000 buildings and structures, valued at $146bn (£89bn). The bases bristle with an inventory of weapons whose worth is measured in the trillions and whose killing power could wipe out all life on earth several times over.

The official figures exclude the huge build-up of troops and structures in Iraq and Afghanistan over the past decade, as well as secret or unacknowledged facilities in Israel, Kuwait, the Philippines and many other places. In just three years of the Iraq and Afghanistan wars, £2bn was spent on military construction. A single facility in Iraq, Balad Airbase, houses 30,000 troops and 10,000 contractors, and extends across 16 square miles, with an additional 12 square mile "security perimeter". From the battle zones of Afghanistan and Iraq to quiet corners of Curaçao, Korea and Britain, the US military domain consists of sprawling army bases, small listening posts, missile and artillery testing ranges and berthed aircraft carriers (moved to "trouble spots" around the world, each carrier is considered by the US navy as "four and a half acres of sovereign US territory"). While the bases are, literally speaking, barracks and weapons depots, staging areas for warmaking and ship repairs, complete with golf courses and basketball courts, they are also political claims, spoils of war, arms sale showrooms and toxic industrial sites. In addition to the cultural imperialism and episodes of rape, murder, looting and land seizure that have always accompanied foreign armies, local communities are now subjected to the ear-splitting noise of jets on exercise, to the risk of helicopters and warplanes crashing into residential areas, and to exposure to the toxic materials that the military uses in its daily operations.

The global expansion of US bases—and with it the rise of the US as a world superpower—is a legacy of the Second World War. In 1938, the US had 14 military bases outside its continental borders. Seven years later, it had 30,000 installations in roughly 100 countries. While this number was projected to shrink to 2,000 by 1948 (following pressure from other nations to return bases in their own territory or colonies, and pressure at home to demobilise the 12-million-man military), the US continued to pursue access rights to land and air space around the world. It established security alliances with multiple states within Europe (Nato), the Middle East and south Asia (Cento) and south-east Asia (Seato), as well as bilateral agreements with Japan, Taiwan, South Korea, Australia and New Zealand. Status of Forces Agreements (Sofas) were crafted in each country to specify what the military could do, and usually gave US soldiers broad immunity from prosecution for crimes committed and environmental damage caused. These agreements and subsequent base operations have mostly been shrouded in secrecy, helped by the National Security Act of 1947. New US bases were built in remarkable numbers in West Germany, Italy, Britain and Japan, with the defeated Axis powers hosting the most significant numbers (at one point, Japan was peppered with 3,800 US installations).

As battles become bases, so bases become battles; the sites in east Asia acquired during the Spanish-American war in 1898 and during the Second World War—such as Guam, Thailand and the Philippines—became the primary bases from which the US waged war on Vietnam. The number of raids over north and south Vietnam required tons of bombs unloaded at the naval station in Guam. The morale of ground troops based in Vietnam, as fragile as it was to become through the latter part of the 1960s, depended on R&R (rest and recreation) at bases outside the country, which allowed them to leave the war zone and yet be shipped back quickly and inexpensively for further fighting. The war also depended on the heroin the CIA was able to ship in to the troops on the battlefield in Vietnam from its secret bases in Laos. By 1967, the number of US bases had returned to 1947 levels.

Technological changes in warfare have had important effects on the configuration of US bases. Long-range missiles and the development of ships that can make much longer runs without resupply have altered the need for a line of bases to move forces forward into combat zones, as has the aerial refuelling of military jets. An arms airlift from the US to the British in the Middle East in 1941–42, for example, required a long hopscotch of bases, from Florida to Cuba, Puerto Rico, Barbados, Trinidad, British Guiana, northeast Brazil, Fernando de Noronha, Takoradi (now in Ghana), Lagos, Kano (now in Nigeria) and Khartoum, before finally making delivery in Egypt. In the early 1970s, US aircraft could make the same delivery with one stop in the Azores, and today can do so non-stop.

On the other hand, the pouring of money into military R&D (the Pentagon has spent more than $85bn in 2009), and the corporate profits to be made in the development and deployment of the resulting technologies, have been significant factors in the ever larger numbers of technical facilities on foreign soil. These include such things as missile early-warning radar, signals intelligence, satellite control and space-tracking telescopes. The will to gain military control of space, as well as gather intelligence, has led to the establishment of numerous new military bases in violation of arms-control agreements such as the 1967 Outer Space Treaty. In Colombia and Peru, and in secret and mobile locations elsewhere in Latin America, radar stations are primarily used for anti-trafficking operations.

Since 2000, with the election of George W Bush and the ascendancy to power of a group of men who believed in a more aggressive and unilateral use of military power (some of whom stood to profit handsomely from the increased military budget that would require), US imperial ambition has grown. Following the declaration of a war on terror and of the right to pre-emptive war, the number of countries into which the US inserted and based troops radically expanded. The Pentagon put into action a plan for a network of "deployment" or "forward operating" bases to increase the reach of current and future forces. The Pentagon-aligned, neoconservative think tank the Project for the New American Century stressed that "while the unresolved conflict with Iraq provides the immediate justification, the need for a substantial American force presence in the Gulf transcends the issue of the regime of Saddam Hussein."

The new bases are designed to operate not defensively against particular threats but as offensive, expeditionary platforms from which military capabilities can be projected quickly, anywhere. The Global Defence Posture Review of 2004 announced these changes, focusing not just on reorienting the footprint of US bases away from cold war locations, but on remaking legal arrangements that support expanded military activities with other allied countries and prepositioning equipment in those countries. As a recent army strategic document notes, "Military personnel can be transported to, and fall in on, prepositioned equipment significantly more quickly than the equivalent unit could be transported to the theatre, and prepositioning equipment overseas is generally less politically difficult than stationing US military personnel."

Terms such as facility, outpost or station are used for smaller bases to suggest a less permanent presence. The US department of defence currently distinguishes between three types of military facility. "Main operating bases" are those with permanent personnel, strong infrastructure, and often family housing, such as Kadena Airbase in Japan and Ramstein Airbase in Germany. "Forward operating sites" are "expandable warm facilit[ies] maintained with a limited US military support presence and possibly prepositioned equipment", such as Incirlik Airbase in Turkey and Soto Cano Airbase in Honduras. Finally, "co-operative security locations" are sites with few or no permanent US personnel, maintained by contractors or the host nation for occasional use by the US military, and often referred to as "lily pads". These are cropping up around the world, especially throughout Africa, a recent example being in Dakar, Senegal.

Moreover, these bases are the anchor—and merely the most visible aspect—of the US military's presence overseas. Every year, US forces train 100,000 soldiers in 180 countries, the presumption being that beefed-up local militaries will help to pursue US interests in local conflicts and save the US money, casualties and bad publicity when human rights abuses occur (the blowback effect of such activities has been made clear by the strength of the Taliban since 9/11). The US military presence also involves jungle, urban, desert, maritime and polar training exercises across wide swathes of landscape, which have become the pretext for substantial and permanent positioning of troops. In recent years, the US has run around 20 exercises annually on Philippine soil, which have resulted in a near-continuous presence of US soldiers in a country whose people ejected US bases in 1992 and whose constitution forbids foreign troops to be based on its territory. Finally, US personnel work every day to shape local legal codes to facilitate US access: they have lobbied, for example, to change the Philippine and Japanese constitutions to allow, respectively, foreign troop basing and a more-than-defensive military.

Asked why the US has a vast network of military bases around the world, Pentagon officials give both utilitarian and humanitarian arguments. Utilitarian arguments include the claim that bases provide security for the US by deterring attack from hostile countries and preventing or remedying unrest or military challenges; that bases serve the national economic interests of the US, ensuring access to markets and commodities needed to maintain US standards of living; and that bases are symbolic markers of US power and credibility—and so the more the better. Humanitarian arguments present bases as altruistic gifts to other nations, helping to liberate or democratise them, or offering aid relief. None of these humanitarian arguments deals with the problem that many of the bases were taken during wartime and "given" to the US by another of the war's victors.

Critics of US foreign policy have dissected and dismantled the arguments made for maintaining a global system of military basing. They have shown that the bases have often failed in their own terms: despite the Pentagon's claims that they provide security to the regions they occupy, most of the world's people feel anything but reassured by their presence. Instead of providing more safety for the US or its allies, they have often provoked attacks, and have made the communities around bases key targets of other nations' missiles. On the island of Belau in the Pacific, the site of sharp resistance to US attempts to instal a submarine base and jungle training centre, people describe their experience of military basing in the Second World War: "When soldiers come, war comes." On Guam, a joke among locals is that few people except for nuclear strategists in the Kremlin know where their island is.

As for the argument that bases serve the national economic interest of the US, the weapons, personnel and fossil fuels involved cost billions of dollars, most coming from US taxpayers. While bases have clearly been concentrated in countries with key strategic resources, particularly along the routes of oil and gas pipelines in central Asia, the Middle East and, increasingly, Africa, from which one-quarter of US oil imports are expected by 2015, the profits have gone first of all to the corporations that build and service them, such as Halliburton. The myth that bases are an altruistic form of "foreign aid" for locals is exploded by the substantial costs involved for host economies and polities. The immediate negative effects include levels of pollution, noise, crime and lost productive land that cannot be offset by soldiers' local spending or employment of local people. Other putative gains tend to benefit only local elites and further militarise the host nations: elaborate bilateral negotiations swap weapons, cash and trade privileges for overflight and land-use rights. Less explicitly, rice imports, immigration rights to the US or overlooking human rights abuses have been the currency of exchange.

The environmental, political, and economic impact of these bases is enormous. The social problems that accompany bases, including soldiers' violence against women and car crashes, have to be handled by local communities without compensation from the US. Some communities pay the highest price: their farmland taken for bases, their children neurologically damaged by military jet fuel in their water supplies, their neighbours imprisoned, tortured and disappeared by the autocratic regimes that survive on US military and political support given as a form of tacit rent for the bases. The US military has repeatedly interfered in the domestic affairs of nations in which it has or desires military access, operating to influence votes and undermine or change local laws that stand in the way.

Social movements have proliferated around the world in response to the empire of US bases, ever since its inception. The attempt to take the Philippines from Spain in 1898 led to a drawn-out guerrilla war for independence that required 126,000 US occupation troops to stifle. Between 1947 and 1990, the US military was asked to leave France, Yugoslavia, Iran, Ethiopia, Libya, Sudan, Saudi Arabia, Tunisia, Algeria, Vietnam, Indonesia, Peru, Mexico and Venezuela. Popular and political objection to the bases in Spain, the Philippines, Greece and Turkey in the 1980s gave those governments the grounds to negotiate significantly more compensation from the US. Portugal threatened to evict the US from important bases in the Azores unless it ceased its support for independence for its African colonies.

Since 1990, the US has been sent packing, most significantly, from the Philippines, Panama, Saudi Arabia, Vieques and Uzbekistan. Of its own accord, for varying reasons, it decided to leave countries from Ghana to Fiji. Persuading the US to clean up after itself—including, in Panama, more than 100,000 rounds of unexploded ordnance—is a further struggle. As in the case of the US navy's removal from Vieques in 2003, arguments about the environmental and health damage of the military's activities remain the centrepiece of resistance to bases.

Many are also concerned by other countries' overseas bases—primarily European, Russian and Chinese—and by the activities of their own militaries, but the far greater number of US bases and their weaponry has understandably been the focus. The sense that US bases represent a major injustice to the host community and nation is very strong in countries where US bases have the longest standing and are most ubiquitous. In Okinawa, polls show that 70 to 80 per cent of the island's people want the bases, or at least the marines, to leave. In 1995, the abduction and rape of a 12-year-old Okinawan girl by two US marines and one US sailor led to demands for the removal of all US bases in Japan. One family in Okinawa has built a large peace museum right up against the edge of the Futenma Airbase, with a stairway to the roof that allows busloads of schoolchildren and other visitors to view the sprawling base after looking at art depicting the horrors of war.

In Korea, the great majority of the population feels that a reduction in US presence would increase national security; in recent years, several violent deaths at the hands of US soldiers triggered vast candlelight vigils and protests across the country. And the original inhabitants of Diego Garcia, evicted from their homes between 1967 and 1973 by the British on behalf of the US for a naval base, have organised a concerted campaign for the right to return, bringing legal suit against the British government, a story told in David Vine's recent book *Island of Shame*. There is also resistance to the

US expansion plans into new areas. In 2007, a number of African nations baulked at US attempts to secure access to sites for military bases. In eastern Europe, despite well-funded campaigns to convince Poles and Czechs of the value of US bases and much sentiment in favour of accepting them in pursuit of closer ties with Nato and the EU, and promised economic benefits, vigorous protests have included hunger strikes and led the Czech government, in March, to reverse its plan to allow a US military radar base to be built in the country.

The US has responded to action against bases with a renewed emphasis on "force protection," in some cases enforcing curfews on soldiers, and cutting back on events that bring local people on to base property. The department of defence has also engaged in the time-honoured practice of renaming: clusters of soldiers, buildings and equipment have become "defence staging posts" or "forward operating locations" rather than military bases. Regulating documents become "visiting forces agreements", not "status of forces agreements," or remain entirely secret. While major reorganisation of bases is under way for a host of reasons, including a desire to create a more mobile force with greater access to the Middle East, eastern Europe and central Asia, the motives also include an attempt to prevent political momentum of the sort that ended US use of the Vieques and Philippine bases.

The attempt to gain permanent basing in Iraq foundered in 2008 on the objections of forces in both Iraq and the US. Obama, in his Cairo speech in June, may have insisted that "we pursue no bases" in either Iraq or Afghanistan, but there has been no sign of any significant dismantling of bases there, or of scaling back the US military presence in the rest of the world. The US secretary of state, Hillary Clinton, recently visited Japan to ensure that it follows through on promises to provide the US with a new airfield on Okinawa and billions of dollars to build new housing and other facilities for 8,000 marines relocating to Guam. She ignored the invitation of island activists to come and see the damage left by previous decades of US base activities. The myriad land-grabs and hundreds of billions of dollars spent to quarter troops around the world persist far beyond Iraq and Afghanistan, and too far from the headlines.

Two Cheers for the US Empire!*

By Thomas Donnelly
New Statesman, August 3, 2009

The argument against US overseas military bases is almost always a sur-rogate argument against the exercise of US power. But you can't have one without the other. And the annoying thing about American *hyperpuissance* is that, compared to other probable outcomes, it produces what appears to be the least bad international system. And so, various allies continue to tolerate, and even encourage, the presence of US military installations in their coun-tries. On 23 July, Iraq's prime minister, Nouri al-Maliki, took the occasion of his first visit to Washington since the election of Barack Obama to signal that he would rather US troops did not withdraw entirely from Iraq in 2011. "If Iraqi forces required further training and further support," he told an audi-ence at the US Institute for Peace, "we shall examine this at that time based on the needs of Iraq." Indeed, the Iraqi prime minister is more enthusiastic about continued American imperialism than is the US president.

Maliki apparently appreciates the realities of geography better than Obama does. The strategic justification for the Iraq pull-back is that US forces will return to their previous posture as "offshore balancers", relying on naval and air strength to tip the balance of power in the greater Middle East. America's allies in east Asia—Japan in particular, but also Australia, which has just pro-duced a defence white paper suggesting a need to "hedge" against the ebbing of US presence in the western Pacific—are experiencing Maliki-like anxieties. For those people who feel themselves most exposed in a dangerous world, the proximity of US forces is apparently comforting.

To be sure, the US military presence is not a free good for these countries. Again, Maliki's very delicate domestic political calculations are illustrative: the line between "occupier" and "strategic partner" is a fine one, but nowhere more so than in Iraq. Nor, from an American standpoint, is having to work with leaders such as Maliki a perfect blessing; through the years the US has made alliances of convenience with some very nasty people.

But that there should be a liberal purpose to statecraft is a rather uniquely Anglo-American, almost Whiggish idea. What is historically distinct about US power is that it correlates quite remarkably with the spread of human liberty and representative government, through time and across cultures. What has been true abroad has also been true at home: the cold war period, so far from producing the feared "garrison state," also brought a dramatic expansion of political rights for African Americans, women and even homosexuals.

And so two cheers for the global exercise of American power and the overseas military bases that are a necessary consequence thereof. Given that lamentably few governments in human history deserve any applause, one can see why not only Americans, but many others around the world think the risks are worth the reward.

The American Non-Empire[*]

By Ed Morrissey
Captain's Quarter, November 27, 2007

The charge of empire-building gets made repeatedly by critics of the United States, to the point where counterargument rarely occurs. This passivity comes in part from the unquestionable international military reach of the US and its commercial, cultural, and political influence around the world. However, the term "empire" means much more than influence and reach, as Jonah Goldberg notes in today's *Los Angeles Times*:

> Critics of American foreign policy point to the fact that the U.S. does many things that empires once did—police the seas, deploy militaries abroad, provide a lingua franca and a global currency—and then rest their case. But noting that X does many of the same things as Y does not mean that X and Y are the same thing. The police provide protection, and so does the Mafia. Orphanages raise children, but they aren't parents. If your wife cleans your home, tell her she's the maid because maids also clean homes. See how well that logic works.
>
> When they speak of the American empire, critics fall back on cartoonish notions, invoking Hollywoodized versions of ancient Rome or mothballed Marxist caricatures of the British Raj. But unlike the Romans or even the British, our garrisons can be ejected without firing a shot. We left the Philippines when asked. We may split from South Korea in the next few years under similar circumstances. Poland wants our military bases; Germany is grumpy about losing them. When Turkey, a U.S. ally and member of NATO, refused to let American troops invade Iraq from its territory, the U.S. government said "fine." We didn't invade Iraq for oil (all we needed to do to buy it was lift the embargo), and we've made it clear that we'll leave Iraq if the Iraqis ask. . . .
>
> America has picked up where the British left off. Whatever sway the U.S. holds over far-flung reaches of the globe is derived from the fact that we have been, and hopefully shall continue to be, the leader of the free world, offering help and guidance, peace and prosperity, where and when we can, as best we can, and asking little in return. If that makes us an empire, so be it. But I think "leader of the free world" is the only label we'll ever need or—one hopes—ever want.

The age of empire has long since passed. Real empires—not the pseudoempire that critics accuse America of building—invaded and colonized territory,

* Originally printed in Captain's Quarters, November 27, 2007. Reprinted with permission of author.

putting them and their peoples under a single head of state, usually a monarchy. The British didn't just have military bases in India for centuries; they occupied it and considered India their property. The Ottoman Empire expanded throughout Southwest Asia through military conquest and ruthless control by the Caliphate.

Our so-called empire has garnered no territory in this manner. As Jonah points out, we have military bases around the world, but they exist at the pleasure of the sovereign governments that control that territory. Even our Guantanamo Bay base exists as a result of an international agreement between Cuba (its previous government) and the US giving us a long-term lease on the property. We do not consider Germany an American colony, and neither does anyone else.

In fact, rather than enriching ourselves, our military bases have made it possible for our allies to prosper through smaller investment in their own militaries. This has led to some economic poor choices and a militarily weak Europe, which was our intent 60 years ago but somewhat of a complication in today's world. Instead of investing in a robust military, these nations have spent their monies on social programs and welfare systems, as well as their own economies.

Cultural and commercial hegemony makes even less sense as empire. No one forces people to buy American—not even in America. The adoption of our entertainment and tastes, to the extent that it happens, is completely voluntary. American military might makes free trade in these areas possible, but it doesn't impose "Seinfeld" on foreigners any more than China imposes T-shirts on Americans.

We have fought and bled and died all over the world, but not for conquest; we have liberated lands from empire, not built our own. As Colin Powell and others have noted, the only land we required was enough to bury our dead. That hardly fits with the notion of imperialism in any real sense, and the accusation of empire insults the memory of those who lie in those graves. It's time we started to make that counterargument.

Obama to Confront Limits of America's Overstretched Military[*]

By Anna Mulrine
U.S. News & World Report, January 16, 2009

With progress in Iraq still precarious and the war in Afghanistan growing ever more violent, the American military remains overburdened and, U.S. officials repeatedly point out, dangerously overstretched. Troops are also exhausted, after back-to-back tours that are leaving a growing number of military families in shambles.

It's hardly an alluring recruiting scenario. But top U.S. military leaders warn that if the Pentagon is to continue to meet its responsibilities around the world, it will need more troops.

"You can't do what we've been asked to do with the number of people we have," Undersecretary of the Army Nelson Ford noted in a recent interview, driving home what has long been conventional wisdom within the halls of the Pentagon: Shortages in the military ranks will be one of the chief national security challenges of the Barack Obama administration.

Indeed, those demands will likely only grow greater under Obama's watch, particularly after his anticipated approval of plans to send 30,000 additional forces to Afghanistan. There, troops will not only be called upon to fight hard against increasingly sophisticated Taliban forces, but they will also need to put expert-level logisticians in place to figure out how to supply this influx of soldiers and marines—what amounts to a doubling of current U.S. force levels.

And even as troops leave Iraq for Afghanistan on the heels of greater stability in Baghdad, the U.S. military will need considerable forces to support the Iraqi military, including supply specialists, aviators, and intelligence officers. "As the [brigade combat teams] draw down, it means you have more people spread thin," Ford noted. "You need more logistics, more aviation, controls, and communication.

"You can see a point," he added, "where it's going to be very difficult to cope."

This comes as little surprise to the Pentagon, which is well underway with a plan to grow the ranks of the Army by 65,000 soldiers by next year, bringing active duty forces to a total of 547,000. The Marine Corps plans to add 27,000 to its ranks, growing to 202,000 by 2011. It's worth noting that the Pentagon recently accelerated those plans—originally the increase was slated to be complete by 2012, rather than the current goal of 2010—in the face of dire demand.

Such growth is expensive. Last year, the Pentagon asked for $15 billion to add 7,000 soldiers and $5 billion to add 5,000 marines to the ranks of the Corps. Separately, the Department of Defense requested an additional $11 billion to cover the costs of retaining, training, and recruiting its forces.

The area of retention is perhaps the greatest staffing concern of top military officials. Troops are tired. Michael O'Hanlon, a senior fellow in foreign policy at the Brookings Institution, a Washington, D.C., think tank, noted in a recent article that 27 percent of soldiers who had completed three or four tours in Iraq showed signs of post-traumatic stress disorder, according to a 2008 survey, versus 12 percent after one tour and 18 percent after two. The figures could be aided by more rest time between tours—at least 18 to 24 months—but it will likely be at least three years, according to top military officials, before troops get more than a year to rest between deployments.

Recruiting, too, has been a considerable challenge for the all-volunteer military engaged in two tough wars. When the Army fell short of its recruiting goals in 2005, it raised the maximum recruiting age to 42 years old, and added sign-up bonuses as high as $40,000. It also began enlisting more recruits with general equivalency degrees rather than high school diplomas. Just over 70 percent of new recruits had high school diplomas in 2007, for example, a 25-year low. Moral waivers for new recruits with criminal histories are also on the rise, nearly doubling from 860 waivers for marines and soldiers convicted of felonies in 2007, up by 400 from 2006. The Pentagon argues that these are modest figures relative to the size of the force, and that 97 percent of Marine Corps recruits in 2008 had high school diplomas.

Even as the military grows, however, top officials are warning that the Pentagon will need still more troops. Ford recently said that the Army will need an additional 30,000 soldiers to fulfill its duties, not only in Iraq and Afghanistan but around the world. Others have noted that U.S. military commands in the North and in Korea are also clamoring for more soldiers. So, too, is the new U.S. Africa Command. Then there are the demands of cyberwarfare, which will need more staff, say officials, after some recent crippling cyberattacks on U.S. computer systems at the Pentagon and at U.S. bases abroad.

As if all these challenges were not enough, the Pentagon instituted new training requirements in December that will require troops to receive instruction in how to do "full spectrum combat." This means, in military parlance, drills in a host of old-school battle scenarios such as, for example, traditional tank wars. Soldiers have spent the last few years focused on counterinsurgency operations, much to the consternation of some who warn that America might one day be drawn into a land battle with another world power. But it already looks like the implementation of that new doctrine will have to be tabled for the next three years, say top military officials, because it will be at least that long before troops have 18 to 24 months between tours, the amount of time required for such training.

The news for military manning isn't all bad, however. The outlook for recruiting is growing steadily sunnier in the wake of the implosion of the U.S. economy, which has been a boon for military recruiters. "We do benefit when things look less positive in civil society," said David Chu, the undersecretary of defense for personnel and readiness. Fiscal year 2008, which ended in September, was the best in five years for the Department of Defense. Top officials remain only cautiously optimistic, however. "Military recruiting is always a challenge," says Curt Gilroy, accession policy director for Defense, "regardless of what the unemployment rate is."

2

Afghanistan: "Graveyard of Empires"?

Editor's Introduction

Toward the end of 2009, public debate centered not on whether the United States should *reduce* its military presence in Afghanistan, but rather whether President Barack Obama should institute a troop "surge," a strategy similar to the one his predecessor, George W. Bush, had used two years earlier to quell violence in Iraq. On December 1, 2009, Obama announced that, over a period of six months, he would send an additional 30,000 troops to Afghanistan. This strategy came in response to what Obama called a "deteriorating" situation: the ousted Taliban regime was regaining strength, and al-Qaeda terrorists continued to take refuge in the mountainous region along the Pakistani border. To underscore the urgency of the mission, Obama also set a timeline for withdrawal, indicating that troops would begin coming home 18 months after the start of the surge.

Obama's plan drew mixed reactions. While many Americans had viewed the Afghanistan conflict as "the good war"—a campaign aimed at punishing the regime that had harbored Osama bin Laden and his fellow 9/11 plotters—mounting casualties and lack of progress were leading some to question the mission. The war's harshest critics argued that Afghanistan would never be stabilized, and that this notorious "graveyard of empires," a vast stretch of land that neither British nor Soviet invaders had been able to conquer, was destined to backslide into chaos.

In light of Obama's decision to proceed with the new strategy, the articles in this chapter present arguments for and against increased troop deployment in Afghanistan. The selections also consider how the U.S. military, regardless of troop level, should conduct operations in the embattled Asian nation. While some contend that force is needed to defeat the Taliban and affirm the legitimacy of President Hamid Karzai's American-backed government, others advocate working with the Afghan people and providing them with the education and basic services they so desperately need.

In the first selection, "The American Awakening," Dexter Filkins claims the Taliban's resurgence was inevitable, since American forces never presented the Afghan people with a viable alternative government. Filkins writes that efforts to replicate the successful Iraqi surge and "Awakening"—the process by which Sunni insurgents turned on al-Qaeda fighters—are unlikely to pan out, given the "deeply atomized" nature of Afghanistan's population. Filkins concludes that the United States' best strategy involves gaining the support of low-level Taliban commanders and "local militiamen" and convincing them to cooperate with the fledgling government. "But all this is not very likely," he writes, "at least not yet."

In "Debating Afghanistan" Paul R. Pillar, director of graduate studies at Georgetown University's Security Studies Program, argues that the United States has little to gain from fighting in Afghanistan, since few al-Qaeda operatives remain in the country. Center for a New American Security president John Nagl takes the opposite position, stressing in his response the importance of defeating the Taliban and preventing Afghanistan from becoming a "safe haven" for terrorists.

The author of "Obama Doesn't Make a Case for More Troops," the next selection, accuses the president of failing "to make a compelling case that an escalation in Afghanistan is vital to core U.S. national interests." The writer posits that winning a guerilla war against the Taliban would take longer than 18 months, and that it ultimately wouldn't be worth the effort, since the most dangerous al-Qaeda terrorists are now based in neighboring Pakistan.

The *Commonweal* editors behind the subsequent article, "Obama's Surge," take a slightly more positive view of the president's plan, calling it "plausible," in the sense that it's modeled after what proved to be an effective strategy in Iraq. Even so, the authors call for "political, not merely military solutions" to the many problems facing Afghanistan, expressing skepticism that 18 months will be enough time to turn things around.

The following selection, "The West Can Encourage Legitimacy and Accountability," finds Aziz Hakimi outlining a four-part plan for winning in Afghanistan. Eschewing military solutions, Hakimi insists the United States needs to promote reconciliation among the nation's warring factions, reform government institutions, provide development aid for citizens, and foster collaboration between civil society groups.

In the final piece, "The Slog of War," Nir Rosen recounts his experiences in Afghanistan, revealing the challenges of counterinsurgency, or COIN, one strategy for defeating the Taliban and al-Qaeda. COIN involves winning the trust of locals and using nonviolent means to weaken the influence of insurgents. Some military officials argue that successful COIN operations require more time and resources than the United States is willing to commit.

The American Awakening[*]

By Dexter Filkins
The New Republic, March 1, 2010

In The Graveyard of Empires: America's War in Afghanistan
By Seth G. Jones
(W.W. Norton, 414 pp., $27.95)

I.

With the war in Afghanistan hanging in the balance, it is useful, if a little sad, to recall just how complete the American-led victory was in the autumn of 2001. By December, the Taliban had vanished from Kabul, Kandahar, and much of the countryside. Afghans celebrated by flinging their turbans and dancing in the streets. They dug up TV sets, wrapped in plastic, from hiding places in their gardens. In Mullah Omar's hometown of Sangesar, the locals broke into his madrassa and tore out the door frames for firewood. Among ordinary Afghans, there was a genuine sense of deliverance. The world, which had abandoned them more than a decade before, was coming back.

What a difference eight years makes. Today the Taliban are fighting more vigorously and in more places than at any point since they fled the capital. They are governing, too, with sharia courts and "shadow" administrators, in large parts of the Pashtun heartland in the south and the east. American soldiers are dying faster than ever: twice as many were killed in 2009 as in 2008. Perhaps most disturbing, the Afghan government of President Hamid Karzai has revealed itself to be a hollow shell, incapable of doing much of anything save rigging elections. The center is giving way.

The catastrophic reversal in Afghanistan has many fathers, but all the many failures can be boiled down to two: a lack of resources, which might have been used to build enduring Afghan institutions; and a conviction, until recently, that time was on our side. In the crucial years from 2002 to 2006, as the fledgling Afghan government hobbled along, the Americans—by this I mean officials in the Bush administration in Washington, for the soldiers and the diplomats in the field were perfectly aware of the dangers—carried on without the slightest sense of urgency. In time, the thinking in Washington went, Afghan democracy and the Afghan state would take hold, and the Taliban would wither away.

Today, in the gloomy winter of 2010, American policy has been almost entirely reversed. For the first time since the war began, the White House is devoting its full attention—and the necessary men and matériel—to drive back the Taliban and create an effective Afghan army and state. The thirty thousand new troops being dispatched by President Obama will bring the American total to around 100,000. Obama has also ordered a crash effort to train and equip 400,000 Afghan soldiers and police, in addition to a novel plan to organize tens of thousands of local militiamen. The U.S. military, meanwhile, has learned from its disastrous early mistakes and reinvented itself. In the villages, American soldiers are carrying out a sophisticated strategy that relegates the killing of insurgents to the lowest tier.

And that brings us to the question of time. The most startling line in Obama's speech at West Point in December was its invocation of an eighteen-month timeline for the maximum deployment of American troops. After that, he said, they would begin to come home. The president announced an escalation and a de-escalation in the same speech. You have the resources now, he seemed to say, but your time is short. In the days that followed, his aides qualified the president's pledge—it's "not a cliff, it's a ramp," Jim Jones, the national security advisor, said. And so it probably would be. But the fact remains that with those crucial sentences, Obama bared his intentions, and even his soul. He does not want to be in Afghanistan. His heart is not in it. To be sure, he is proceeding with the escalation, and his heart may yet change, but it is difficult to imagine that the Taliban—and the Pakistanis—have not concluded that the Americans will soon be gone.

After eight years, some Americans may be forgiven for forgetting why the United States went to Afghanistan in the first place. It is important to begin the analysis at the beginning. We invaded Afghanistan following the attacks on September 11, so as to destroy the Taliban and the Al Qaeda leaders and cadres who had taken refuge there. And we succeeded, at least initially. Al Qaeda was all but decapitated. (In December 2001, I walked through several abandoned Al Qaeda safe houses in Kabul.) The Taliban were dead or dispersed. It was the follow-through that proved disastrous.

Seth G. Jones's book provides a vivid sense of just how paltry and misguided the American effort has been. Jones—a scholar at the RAND Corporation and a consultant to the American command in Kabul—chronicles, year by year, the principal American and NATO failures over the course of the war. Reading *In the Graveyard of Empires* is an experience in dramatic irony: you know the glorious beginning, you know the dismal present; so you watch the American-led project in Afghanistan unravel with a tightened stomach and clenched teeth. But if we are ever to redeem the Afghan venture—and the consequences of failure seem catastrophic—*In the Graveyard of Empires* will help to show what might still be done to build something enduring in Afghanistan and finally allow the U.S. to go home.

What Jones demonstrates so persuasively—and what many of Obama's homebound critics have often missed—is that for the past eight years, the trouble in Afghanistan has been less the presence of American and Western troops than their absence. This, and their utter failure to build any sort of institutions that might take their place. It was these two factors, more than any others, that made possible the return of the Taliban. Owing to the pathetic resources devoted to the endeavor, the Americans and NATO were never able to protect the Afghan people—not from crime, not from corrupt officials, not from insurgents. The government and the security forces they built and trained were never able to do it for them. The Taliban, which Jones acutely describes as "a complex adaptive system," brought itself back to life and flowed into the breach.

From the beginning, the Bush administration justified the "light footprint" as a way of not stoking Afghan nationalism—despite the overwhelming evidence that ordinary Afghans thirsted for foreign help in the wake of the Taliban's collapse. Their country, after all, was totally destroyed, with no means of repairing itself. As the Taliban regrouped, the Americans and NATO found themselves mounting operations to clear villages and towns of Taliban fighters, only to leave and watch them return. Then the American and NATO troops would go in again. "Mowing the grass," Jones called it. The result was that ordinary Afghans typically encountered American or NATO troops only during military sweeps. And in the early years those American troops were every bit as heavy-handed as their countrymen in Iraq—and the air strikes they called in were even worse. The result was a deep mistrust of the American and NATO militaries, and a growing unwillingness to confront the Taliban.

But the more shocking sin—the inexcusable one—was the failure to build even the rudiments of an enduring Afghan state, one that could provide security for its people and deliver basic public services such as health care and roads. (It is also worth mentioning, to those hankering for an American withdrawal, that a viable Afghan army and police force would likely be the only thing that could prevent a repeat of the horrific civil war that engulfed the country in 1990s.) A functioning Afghan state, as Jones makes painfully clear, might well have gained the allegiance of the Afghan people, even the Pashtuns in the south. What the Afghans got instead was a pathetic principality in Kabul with virtually no capacity to deliver anything outside the city limits.

The central administration that existed in Kabul quickly evolved into a criminal enterprise, siphoning tens of millions of Western dollars and, later, enriching itself from the booming trade in opium. In the countryside, there was, in effect, no government at all: in the early years officials in the Bush administration were only too happy to turn back to the warlords—almost universally reviled by ordinary Afghans—to provide what governance there was. Faced with anarchy in their villages and corruption in their government, Afghans in the south and the east turned to the Taliban. "In short," Jones remarks, "there was a supply of disgruntled locals because of the collapse of Afghan governance, and a demand for recruits by ideologically motivated insurgent leaders. This combination proved deadly." By and large, ordinary Afghans embraced the Taliban not out of some visceral hatred of Westerners, but because they concluded that they had no other choice.

That last point is crucial, especially now. Measuring public opinion in Afghanistan is tricky, but every recent independent poll attempted there shows widespread support for Western troops. They are certainly more popular than the Taliban. By and large, Afghans reserve their fiercest contempt for their own government, which they regard as incompetent and crooked.

My own recent experience is anecdotal but instructive. Last summer, on a foot patrol with a group of American Marines in Helmand Province, we came to a village named Mian Poshteh, where the locals actually lined up to watch a Taliban ambush, which they knew was on the way. As the Marines worked their way down a trail, a huge homemade bomb, hidden in the sand, exploded. The bomb blew a hundred feet into the air and a dozen Marines disappeared inside the cloud. Miraculously, none of them died; the bomber had pulled his trigger a few seconds too soon. But when the marines ventured to the outskirts of Mian Poshteh and made their inquiries, not a single Afghan would tell them a thing. "Maybe they came at night," a man named Assadullah said with a shrug.

Yet my experience that day in Mian Poshteh was exceptional. Over several days of walking the Helmand River Valley, my best sense was that the locals, more than anything, felt trapped—caught unhappily between the Taliban, whom they feared, and the Americans and the Afghans of Karzai's government, whom they distrusted. And wherever the Americans demonstrated that they intended to stay—and that they intended to help build a government—the Afghans proved remarkably receptive.

A few days after the bomb attack, I sat with a group of Marines under the shade of a eucalyptus tree listening to Gul Jan, the elder in the village of Jan Mohammed Khel. For more than an hour we sat and drank tea while Jan explained his village's predicament. Unlike Mian Poshteh, Jan Mohammed Khel fell within a six-mile-long area secured by the Americans, dubbed the "snake's head" for its oblong shape. In two years, the Americans had raised up a local government, a small police force, and a small base with about three hundred Afghan soldiers. Most important, about three hundred American Marines had hunkered down and stayed there, and in an area small enough that they could control it. The Taliban were still active inside the "snake's head," but security inside the villages improved a lot.

Sitting under the eucalyptus tree, Jan seemed relaxed enough to speak his mind. The story he told was all too sadly believable. "All my life, I have seen destruction," Jan said. The village's single school was burned by the Taliban three years before, he said, and most of the canals had been damaged by fighting. What Jan and the rest of the villagers—about fifty young men sat with us—wanted was peace, and a government that could enforce it. The Taliban, he said, came and went by force, without much enthusiasm from the locals. "They are like shadows," Jan said. "They come in the night, they do their things, and then they are gone."

Jan was unambiguous about his preferences. "If we had security, we could get rid of them," he said of the Taliban. "But how can we fight them? This kind of disease is hard to get rid of." The only people strong enough to expel the Taliban, Jan said, were the Americans. "Our government is very weak. I am sorry to tell you this, but you can't go now. First there must be security, and then you can go." And he added: "You shouldn't stay forever. You have your own country to go to."

Were Jan and the other Afghans like him lying to the Americans to buy themselves a little peace? Maybe. Just two days before, not a mile from Jan's village, an American patrol had been struck by a bomb. At the very least, Jan probably knows people in the Taliban, and maybe even allows them to use his village. Still, my strong impression was that Jan and other Afghans like him—not far away, on yet another foot patrol, an Afghan man had come out of his house to warn the Marines of a pending Taliban ambush—were speaking the truth. In the hour-long conversation with Jan, neither he nor any of the other Afghan men who gathered to speak with me exhibited the slightest trace of hostility or fear.

What does such an encounter mean for the United States and its NATO allies? It means, for one thing, that many Afghans, even in the worst places, are still receptive to their presence. It means that the Afghans' ultimate allegiance is probably still up for grabs. It means that the U.S. and NATO forces are not, in most places, regarded as an occupying army. And it means that if the Americans and NATO practice their counterinsurgency strategy as well as they preach it—that is, if they make protecting the Afghan people their overriding objective—then they have a chance to begin isolating the Taliban from the villages where they operate.

II.

That is the good news. The bad news is that isolating the Taliban and wooing ordinary Afghans may be the easiest task that confronts the United States and its allies. The rest is immeasurably harder.

In the villages along the Helmand River, the principal challenge that awaits the Americans is as clear as the empty winter sky. There are no Afghan institutions—not the army, not the police, not the government—that could take over if the United States and its allies decided to leave. In Mian Poshteh, a scattering of mud huts and cornfields, there were no schools, no paved roads, no police, no electricity, no running water, and only a handful of Afghan soldiers. In this regard, Mian Poshteh is not exceptional in any way.

There is, of course, a central government in Kabul. And what a government it is! Its reach extends outside the capital in only the most notional way. In some of the contested provinces, there is little more than a skeletal administration: a governor, whose life and livelihood is guarded by NATO or Afghan troops, and a handful of terrified Afghans around him. That is pretty much it. In the districts, there is, at least in theory, a local administrator— appointed by the provincial governor, who is appointed by Karzai—but in contested areas such as the provinces of Helmand and Kandahar and Khost, there is often not even that.

And then there is the army and police. There are currently about ninety thousand of each. This is a woefully inadequate number. (Iraq, with a smaller population, has security forces that number about 600,000.) When you consider that an Afghan army and police force are the only things that would ultimately allow the United States to leave here in a good way, it makes you wonder what on earth the Bush administration was doing for the past eight years. President Obama has promised to expand their numbers to at least 400,000, but the more worrisome issue is not their number but their quality.

For the Afghan security forces really are in a sorry state. Eight years into the war, the Afghan army and police have shown themselves willing to fight, but incapable of much more than that: maintaining themselves in the field, mounting operations at night, operating weapons more complicated than a rifle. Even after years of training, the skills and the literacy levels necessary to administer forces in the field have failed to materialize. When it comes to paying, feeding, and supplying soldiers, and tracking who is on leave and who is injured, most Afghan units perform miserably. These tasks are almost always performed by American or NATO soldiers.

Last year, Major General Richard Formica, who was then overseeing the training of the Afghan security forces, spoke to me about the difficulties of creating an army in a country where only one in four adults is literate. "What percentage of police recruits can read?" Formica asked when we met at his headquarters in Kabul. "When I was down in Helmand, where the Brits were training police officers, they said not only could none of them read but they didn't understand what a classroom was. How can you train officers if they can't write arrest reports?"

And then there is Karzai's government in Kabul. On most days, it shows itself to be a spectacularly corrupt institution, existing for little more than its own enrichment. The evidence of its corruption is everywhere. Provincial police chief jobs cost as much as $50,000, with the idea being that the investment will more than pay for itself. The bloated mansions in the Kabul neighborhood called Sherpur, with their dozen-plus bedrooms, sell for millions of dollars each—this in one of the world's poorest countries—and some of them are occupied by current and former officials in Karzai's government.

There appear to be few transactions in public life that have not been overwhelmed by graft. Stand outside the municipal courthouse in Kabul, as I did, and you can talk to any number of people who will tell you about their recent purchases: hearings, judges, verdicts, settlements. At the checkpoints that mark virtually every traffic intersection in the capital, the police regularly demand bribes to let drivers through. It is not uncommon for drivers taking their trucks through the city to fork over money at two dozen posts. I paid a bribe just to walk inside Kabul International Airport.

And then, of course, there was August's presidential election. By the cautious estimates of international observers, Karzai's supporters—that is, his government and the election workers under his command—falsified nearly a million ballots on his behalf. The vote-stealing was astonishingly brazen. In the Shorabak region of Kandahar Province, Karzai loyalists detained the district governor (whom I interviewed) and effectively cancelled the election. Inside Shorabak's local government office, Karzai supporters—otherwise known as election workers—falsified 23,900 ballots and sent them to Kabul. Every one of them was a vote for Karzai.

Much of the vote-stealing appears to have been orchestrated by Ahmed Wali Karzai, the president's brother, who wields power over southern Afghanistan like one of Coppola's godfathers. (It was on his orders that the district governor of Shorabak was detained, I was told.) American officials believe that Ahmed Wali Karzai is deeply involved in the opium trade, which is one of the economic engines of the Taliban. American diplomats and generals have pushed President Karzai to remove him, but so far Karzai has refused.

As the corruption in the Karzai government has grown more blatant, a popular hypothesis has emerged to explain it: that officials in Karzai's government orchestrated the fraud in order to preserve their hold on the moneymaking apparatus that the government has become. "It's a moneymaking machine," one senior American official told me. How do you reform something like this?

Since 2001, President Karzai and his cohorts have known only too well that they have the Americans over a barrel. No matter how hard the Americans pushed him, Karzai could figure, they were not going to leave. In any event, they were never going to do anything that would substantially weaken Karzai himself. And so, in fact, they have not. The Americans have threatened Karzai and cajoled him, and Karzai has laughed behind their backs. Just after the election, the American ambassador, Karl Eikenberry, reportedly went to Karzai and demanded that his brother be sent away from Kandahar. Even this request Karzai refused.

This brings us to President Obama's eighteen-month deadline for U.S. military involvement in Afghanistan. The president obviously was thinking politically: he intended to reassure American voters that his commitment to Afghanistan was not foolishly open-ended. But Obama was also conveying a message to Karzai. With that rather short deadline, Obama seemed to be calling Karzai's bluff. You don't think we'll leave? Just watch. The trouble with Obama's deadline is that, in crucial ways, it appears to be at war with itself. If the intent of the president's message was to convey to the American people that the end was in sight, then it was almost certainly untrue. In all likelihood, the end of America's involvement in Afghanistan is not in sight. Constructing an Afghan state that can stand on its own—an army and a police force, at the very least—will take many years. It will certainly take longer than eighteen months. Obama no doubt recognizes this. But the real trouble with Obama's speech was not its message to the American people, but its message to the Taliban. Can the insurgents really be turned that quickly?

III.

Around the U.S. military's headquarters in downtown Kabul, it is commonplace to hear that Afghanistan, whatever else it is, is not Iraq. Everything here, it is said over and over, is different: the people, the terrain, the language, the insurgency. So it is. And yet at the same time you can sense a yearning among many officers here that, if we are lucky, Afghanistan may turn out to be like Iraq after all.

It may seem odd to place your hopes for winning in Afghanistan on what transpired over the past seven years in Iraq. The latter, of course, was a bloody catastrophe, at least in the first four years. By late 2006, the American invasion had midwifed the implosion of an entire society, a civil war, and a seemingly hopeless military quagmire. But the incontrovertible fact is that then the war turned. To anyone who spent time in Iraq during the nightmare years, the idea that Iraq was headed for anything other than a total disintegration—and the region for a wider war—would have been regarded as fanciful. But for a variety of reasons, not the least of which was luck, the Americans reeled Iraq back in. The bloody streets went pretty still. And despite predictions to the contrary, the relative calm that took hold in late 2007 has largely held. The worst has been avoided.

There is no question that the military's best officers feel humbled by the calamities of Iraq. It is also true that those same officers learned from their mistakes—and that their learning curve helped to pull Iraq back from the abyss. There are not many institutions left in American life that seem capable of such growth, or of such character. And whatever the senior officers are saying, they appear to be banking that a similar set of dynamics will rescue them in Afghanistan. The biggest lesson, as General McChrystal himself told me, was never to give up: "One of the big takeaways from Iraq was that you have to not lose confidence in what you are doing. We were able to go to the edge of the abyss without losing hope."

In Iraq a whole array of things turned, and at the just the right time. Al Qaeda overreached, finally pushing ordinary Sunnis—even insurgents—to open revolt. The training of the Iraqi army and police finally started to jell. The widespread ethnic cleansing of Iraq's cities, principally Baghdad, made the Sunnis fearful of a genocide and easier, in their enclaves, to defend. Iraq's Shia majority recognized that unchallenged power was within its grasp if the Americans could be persuaded to leave. And of course there was the surge.

Two of these phenomena are particularly relevant to the Afghan war: the surge and the Awakening. The Afghan version of the surge was announced by Obama last December. And for all the talk of counterinsurgency, the real hope, clearly, is that the fresh infusion of troops will be able to bleed the Taliban enough to force them to consider some sort of political settlement. This is really the heart of the matter. But how likely is it? Over the course of the past several months, there have been intensifying efforts to reach out to Taliban senior leaders like Mullah Omar. These talks, so far as I can tell, do not appear to have gotten much traction. The Americans insist that Omar disavow Al Qaeda, while the Taliban insist that the Americans leave, or at least set a timetable to leave. Theoretically, at least, it is possible to imagine the basis of a deal based on those positions, particularly if Obama is already intending some sort of drawdown.

But there is the time paradox again. With an eighteen-month deadline looming, what incentive does the Taliban have to make a deal? If you read the movement's regular Internet communiqués, you will see that their morale is not that of an army on the brink of defeat. "With their own hands the Americans made the people of Helmand stand with the holy warriors, and all of them have entered the trenches of resistance to seek vengeance and jihad," a recent Taliban missive proclaimed. "This will bear no fruit except the enemy's defeat, Allah willing." It appears the Taliban wholly expect the Americans to run out of will.

It is here, perhaps, that the experience in Iraq merges with the hope in Afghanistan. In a slightly different way, the Americans are attempting to replicate not just the surge but also the Awakening, the Sunni tribal revolt against Al Qaeda in Mesopotamia. They intend to make deals not with the top of the insurgency, but with the bottom. Beginning in late 2006, American officers and intelligence agents, by cutting deals with tribal leaders, effectively removed thousands of insurgents from the battlefield. Many of them—thirty thousand in all—were put on the American payroll. All of them turned on Al Qaeda.

No one in Kabul really believes that they will be able to produce results as dramatic as those that unfolded in the Awakening in Iraq. In Afghanistan, the old tribal hierarchies are nowhere near as coherent as they are in Iraq. Thirty years of war and Taliban cooptation (in some cases subtle, in some cases brutal) has made it far less likely that the insurgents can be separated from the rest of Afghan society. Afghanistan is a deeply atomized place. It is this fragmentation, more than any other factor, that makes any sort of broad-based settlement difficult to imagine.

Where does that leave the Americans? As one senior American official told me recently, "We are trying everything—and its opposite." But in fact things are not that desperate. Basically, the Americans are hoping they can begin peeling off individual Taliban commanders at the bottom of the food chain, offering them jobs and security if they come along. And they are hoping to hire tens of thousands of local militiamen to defend their own communities. (Ideally, these two initiatives will complement each other.) Over time, the thinking goes, these initiatives could amount to a political settlement, if informal and piecemeal. And things might even go further. It is not inconceivable that the Afghan government could strike deals with Taliban "shadow governors" who are now in effective control of several areas in the south and the east. That would begin to look very much like the Awakening.

But all this is not very likely, at least not yet. The Taliban would have to be substantially weakened, and the government in Kabul substantially strengthened, for anything like this to take hold in more than a few areas. The Iraq analogy is useful again. There the military hung in, and got it right, and also got lucky. In some ways, really, they got a miracle. But strategies and policies generally do not deliver miracles. Can we expect a miracle in Afghanistan? Of course not. But it may take a miracle for us, and Afghanistan, to win.

Debating Afghanistan*

Paul R. Pillar and John Nagl
National Interest, March/April 2010

Is Afghanistan the Right War?

No: Paul Pillar

The attempted bombing in December of a Detroit-bound airliner, which received as much attention in the United States as any terrorist incident since 9/11, raises the question of why the biggest thing the White House currently is doing in the name of counterterrorism is a counterinsurgency in Afghanistan. The would-be bomber was a Nigerian, radicalized while a student in the United Kingdom and further influenced by an extremist imam in Yemen who had spent half his life in the United States. The plot had nothing to do with Afghanistan. Umar Farouk Abdulmutallab was outfitted with his explosive underwear by a group of Saudis and Yemenis, none of whom was taking orders from anyone hiding in the hinterland of South Asia, even if they figured it was advantageous to adopt the al-Qaeda brand name. The link was ideological, and the ideology will persist whether those in the borderlands of AfPak are dead or alive.

Eight years ago, the United States led a just intervention in the Afghan civil war as a direct response to 9/11. After ousting the Taliban from power and rousting its al-Qaeda friends from Afghanistan, the United States—disquieted by a sense of having abandoned the country after stoking the war against the Soviets—did not declare victory and return home. Now Americans have a president who, after admirably having opposed the misadventure in Iraq from the beginning, is demonstrating his, and the Democratic Party's, toughness and counterterrorist bona fides in the so-called "good war." This is the wrong decision.

It would be fruitless to search the contours of current international terrorism for a compelling explanation of why the United States is escalating a military campaign in Afghanistan. Clearly there is a disconnect between where war is being waged and where terrorism is rearing its ugly head. The appropriate response is not to run off, guns blazing, to find new battlefields, be they in Yemen or anywhere else. The U.S. military, pressing the limits of sustainability and winding up one war while slowly winding down another, does not have the resources to open a new front in every territory that may become associated with terrorism. There is no shortage of such places.

Regardless of the available resources, it is a mistake to think of counterterrorism primarily, as Americans have become wont to do, as the application of military force to particular pieces of real estate. This pattern of thinking is rooted in a history in which the vanquishing of threats to U.S. security has consisted chiefly of armed expeditions to conquer or liberate foreign territory. The pattern has been exacerbated by the unfortunate "war on terror" terminology, which confuses and conflates the seriousness of, the nature of and the means used to counter the threat.

The strength of a terrorist adversary, al-Qaeda or any other, does not correlate with control of a piece of territory in Afghanistan or elsewhere. If a terrorist group has a physical safe haven available, it will use it. But of all the assets that make a group a threat—including ideological appeal and a supply of already-radicalized recruits—occupation of acreage is one of the least important. Past terrorist attacks, including 9/11 (most of the preparations for which took place in scattered locations in the West), demonstrate this.

Although the popular desire to strike forcefully at America's enemies seems to have placed military force front and center in the counterterrorist toolbox, the same basic principles apply to it as to any other tool. Each has its uses but also its limitations, and none can strike a knockout blow. And military force also has downsides: monetary and human costs; collateral damage; and the potential to be counterproductive. The principal barrier to the effective use of bombs and guns in a battle against extremism is the paucity of good military targets involving terrorist operations against the United States—all the more so given that most related activity takes place in apartments, schools or mosques in Western cities.

These limitations are particularly apparent in Afghanistan. Most obvious is that the arch-enemy, al-Qaeda, isn't even there—except, National Security Adviser James Jones tells us, for fewer than a hundred members. So we have adopted the Afghan Taliban as a surrogate enemy. This surrogacy might seem to make sense given that the Taliban has shared an extreme ideology and a past alliance with al-Qaeda. But the Taliban is not a transnational terrorist group. Its goals are not those of Osama bin Laden. It is one of the most insular bands ever to get international attention. It cares about the political and social order in its own country. It does not care about the United States except insofar as we get in the way of its aspirations for the domestic ordering of Afghanistan.

If the Taliban was to return to power, it would see little or no advantage in again harboring a significant presence of bin Laden's al-Qaeda. Its previous host-playing led directly after 9/11 to the biggest setback the Taliban ever suffered. Bin Laden and his partner Ayman al-Zawahiri also would see little to be gained in restoring the previous arrangement. They have successfully hidden in Pakistan for nearly a decade; a return to Afghanistan would only expose them, or their underlings, to uninhibited U.S. firepower, even if U.S. troops were not on the ground.

The counterproductive aspects of applying U.S. military power in Afghanistan also have become all too clear. The foreign military occupation has helped to unite, motivate and win support for the disparate elements we have come to label the Afghan Taliban. The occupation and the inevitable collateral damage and civilian casualties have drained much of what had been—remarkably so for a Muslim country—a reservoir of goodwill toward the United States. Now more Afghans have taken up arms against coalition forces. Many of those who have joined the fight have no sympathy for the Taliban's ideology and do not even warrant the label.

The weakness of the rationale for pressing the fight in Afghanistan has led many supporters of that war to say that the real concern is next door in Pakistan. Visions of mad mullahs getting their hands on Pakistani nuclear weapons are tossed about, but exactly how events in Afghanistan would influence the future of Pakistan does not get explained. The connection seems to be based on simple spatial thinking about instability spreading across borders, rather like the Cold War imagery of red paint oozing over the globe. A Taliban victory in Afghanistan would not bring any significant new resources to bear on conflict in Pakistan, which has a population five times as large and an economy ten times as big as its South Asian neighbor. Nor would it offer Pakistani militants a safe haven any more attractive or useful than the one they already have in Pakistan's own Federally Administered Tribal Areas.

Pakistanis themselves offer the most authoritative take on how, if at all, U.S. military operations in Afghanistan affect security challenges within their own country. The Pakistanis have expressed concern that to the degree those operations are successful, they will merely push militants across the Durand Line (just as bin Laden and his colleagues were pushed across eight years ago). The unpopularity among most Pakistanis of any U.S. military operations in the region also limits Islamabad's political ability to cooperate with the United States in pursuing Washington's goals, including counterterrorist objectives.

Then there is what Pakistani officials do not acknowledge: their continued dalliance with the Afghan Taliban, which they see not as a threat but instead as an asset and a form of insurance against the political uncertainty of Afghanistan. This is the ultimate irony of the U.S. war: the government we are supposedly trying to save from spreading instability is doing business with the enemy we are fighting.

Based on accepted counterinsurgency doctrine, there are ample reasons to be skeptical that the counterinsurgency in Afghanistan will succeed. One is the corruption and illegitimacy of the central government. Another is the possible insufficiency of counterinsurgent forces, given the size of the task at hand. Yet another is the lack of time, given the Obama administration's schedule (politically necessary to reassure Americans the war will not continue indefinitely), by which the U.S. presence will begin to ramp down barely a year after it ramps up.

Whether the counterinsurgency succeeds or fails, however, is not even the main issue in judging whether the war in Afghanistan is worth fighting. The focus on counterinsurgency is a classic case of goal substitution—of dwelling on an intermediate objective while losing sight of why we are pursuing it in the first place. Even if General Stanley McChrystal and the brave and resourceful troops under his command work enough magic to stabilize most of the country and the Karzai government that is supposed to be running it, the large expenditure of blood and treasure will have bought Americans little or nothing in increased safety from terrorist attacks. A successful counterinsurgency would not eliminate the terrorist haven in Pakistan (or even preclude one in unsecured portions of Afghanistan). And it would not address the radicalizing influences and operational preparations in Yemen, Europe, the United States and elsewhere that have far more to do with how many Americans will fall victim to terrorism.

Yes: John Nagl

The United States is "at war against al-Qaeda." So said President Obama in the wake of the attempted Christmas bombing of Northwest Flight 253, and so we are, and so we are likely to be—for many years to come. Afghanistan is one of the critical battlefields in this war; while winning in Afghanistan would not by itself defeat al-Qaeda, losing in Afghanistan would materially strengthen it and prolong the fight, potentially at the cost of many more American lives. This fact may be unpalatable, but it is also inescapable.

This was not a war we planned to fight. Many ignored the early warning signs of a violent threat that would soon pull us deep into conflict. Hardly a non-terrorism-expert eye even blinked when Osama bin Laden announced in the World Islamic Front statement "Jihad Against Jews and Crusaders" in 1998:

> We—with Allah's help—call on every Muslim who believes in Allah and wishes to be rewarded to comply with Allah's order to kill the Americans and plunder their money wherever and whenever they find it. We also call on Muslim ulema, leaders, youths, and soldiers to launch the raid on Satan's U.S. troops and the devil's supporters allying with them, and to displace those who are behind them so that they may learn a lesson.

Yet, the war had arguably been going on for years. It started with the first attack on the World Trade Center in 1993. It continued with an attack on the USS *Cole* docked off Yemen in 2000. And it became unmistakable on September 11, 2001. America's subsequent counterattack on al-Qaeda's base of operations in Afghanistan pushed al-Qaeda's leadership across the Durand Line into Pakistan, where it remains today. We have diminished its ranks through drone strikes and an increasingly aggressive Pakistani counterinsurgency (COIN) campaign.

Now, al-Qaeda has only a minimal presence in Afghanistan, perhaps one hundred or so fighters, which leads many to question why the United States needs to pour more money and more troops into this war effort. Indeed, it is the Taliban—which rose to power in Afghanistan in the late 1990s and provided the shelter from which bin Laden's group planned and executed the September 11 attack—that is now America's main adversary on the ground in Afghanistan. But were the Taliban to regain control of the country, al-Qaeda would simply have more room in which to entrench itself.

Unfortunately, being at war with a nonstate actor like al-Qaeda gives war fighting a whole new complexity for a great power like the United States. Al-Qaeda holds no permanent territory. Its soldiers do not wear uniforms or obey (or even acknowledge) the laws of war. And it specializes in attacking innocent civilians in spectacular displays that attempt to change our behavior through shock-and-awe tactics. It has found innovative means by which to extend its influence, enfranchising associated militant movements across the greater Middle East, and using the Internet to radicalize potential followers and attract recruits—even within America's borders.

Thus, despite substantial progress, the war is not over. One of the lessons of the past eight years is that al-Qaeda will take advantage of safe havens wherever they arise; were the Taliban to regain control of Afghanistan, al-Qaeda would once again have an entire country potentially at its disposal from which to train, plan and operate. And this would only give our enemy greater capability to threaten the United States.

Expelled from Afghanistan within months of 9/11, the Taliban has been gaining strength every year since 2002. The Obama administration has decided that it will nearly triple the number of U.S. forces in Afghanistan; already, in 2009, it invested more in lives and treasure there than it spent in Iraq. Costly as these decisions are—and will be, throughout the rest of Obama's term and likely beyond it—the president effectively had no choice. Much of southern and eastern Afghanistan is now ruled by a shadow Taliban government, in some places even with established courts, a sign of near-total control. Withdrawing from Afghanistan would lead to the rapid demise of the Karzai government, at least in the areas already being wrested from its grasp. The Afghan army and police, developed at enormous expense over the past five years, would crumble without U.S. support.

This is not to mention the regional consequences of an American withdrawal from Afghanistan, the costs of which would be severe. The dominant regional narrative—that the United States will abandon its friends without compunction—would be reinforced, NATO, having made a more extensive commitment to Afghanistan than to any post-Cold War conflict, would be severely weakened. Pakistan would be forced to recalculate its recent decisions to fight against the Taliban inside its own borders because the balance of power in the region would shift in favor of the Taliban upon our departure. Al-Qaeda would likely again decide that Afghanistan presents a more favorable home under those circumstances than do the tribal regions of Pakistan, which are subject to at least some degree of state control. America would again have to invade and occupy Afghanistan to drive out the terrorists.

Counterinsurgency in Afghanistan is the least bad of the options available. And it is a necessity. That does not mean that the United States has to practice large-scale COIN in every failed or failing state where al-Qaeda finds a toehold. Afghanistan is an extreme case—a true failed state that needed its governance and security institutions rebuilt from the ground up, whose neighbor possesses both nuclear weapons and an insurgency of its own, and that is some six hundred miles from the nearest coastline accessible by the U.S. Navy. In other places where al-Qaeda is taking root, less intensive counterinsurgency with a lighter footprint is a viable option. Yemen is a good example of a country where strikes against terrorists, training and equipping host-nation security forces with small numbers of U.S. Special Forces, and economic and governance aid have a good chance of reducing al-Qaeda's presence. But Afghanistan and Pakistan are the core of the problem, the home base of al-Qaeda, with which we are at war. Ceding the battlefield closest to the enemy's capital is no way to win.

We waited until 2009 to give the Afghan conflict the resources success will require. Over the next five years, it should be possible to build an Afghan government that can outperform the Taliban and an Afghan army that can outfight it, especially with the support of a Pakistani government that continues its own efforts on its side of the Durand Line.

The cost of success will be high—higher than it would have been had we not prematurely turned our attention from the war of necessity in Afghanistan to the war of choice in Iraq in 2003. It will put additional strain on our all-volunteer army that was not designed to fight two protracted wars, and, of course, on a military that was hoping for something of a break in the wake of the "surge" of forces into Iraq.

We need a bigger army, and in a period of double-digit unemployment, building up our armed forces is the right choice. An increase of one hundred thousand troops in the army would provide sufficient strength to bring the force back to a more sustainable rotation schedule; the cost would be substantial, but could be paid for by a national-security tax on gasoline. American flags on petrol pumps, thanking the American people for their quarter-a-gallon contribution to the war against al-Qaeda, are a much more patriotic indication of support for the troops than lapel pins—and would also encourage conservation of a natural resource that will grow increasingly scarce in years to come.

The United States is at war with al-Qaeda, and with those who support al-Qaeda. Success will take a toll on us and our Afghan partners. However, the cost of failure in Afghanistan would be even higher.

Before we decide to abandon the nascent democracy in Kabul, turning our back on our more than forty ISAF allies working to stabilize the region, we should give the new commander in Afghanistan a reasonable opportunity to put time-tested counterinsurgency techniques to work.

St. Augustine taught us that the only purpose of war is to build a better peace. After fighting a war to expel the Soviet Union from Afghanistan, we failed to build a better peace there, and we have paid a heavy price for our neglect. We have yet to create an Afghan state that can stand on its own, does not harbor terror and will not destabilize the region. America must not make the mistake of abandoning Afghanistan again—the stakes are far too high.

Pillar Responds

So much seems to flow, naturally and effortlessly, from pinning the label "war" on an endeavor. The term evokes images of a single and clearly identifiable enemy and of military force as the main instrument for defeating that enemy. John Nagl beats the "this is war" drum loudly and embellishes it with references to the "home base" of al-Qaeda and the need to fight close to the "enemy's capital."

This is argument by labeling. It pretends that by affixing a word, certain realities follow. They do not. South Asia is not the "home base" of al-Qaeda, which consists largely of Arab interlopers. No terrorist group has a "capital." Nor is there a single enemy. Al-Qaeda—the group led by Osama bin Laden and holed up in South Asia—has not been organizing most of the terrorism in recent years, even if some of the organizers have chosen to fly the al-Qaeda flag. Nagl sometimes seems to want to go beyond that one enemy, as in referring to the attack on the World Trade Center in 1993. That was perpetrated not by al-Qaeda but instead by other Islamists whose only safe haven was New Jersey.

Nagl assumes rather than establishes that if the Taliban prevails in Afghanistan, then al-Qaeda will rebuild a presence there, and that such a presence would make the group a greater threat. He says nothing to support the first contention; and on the second, only that Afghanistan is a big country and al-Qaeda would have "more room," without explaining exactly what it would do in that space that it cannot and does not already do in other ways and in other places.

This also ignores how circumstances have drastically changed since al-Qaeda's earlier time in Afghanistan. In the 1990s, there was sufficient intelligence and offshore firepower but insufficient political will to damage that presence heavily. When President Clinton ordered cruise-missile strikes against an al-Qaeda camp in 1998, he was accused—even though two U.S. embassies had been attacked—of trying to divert attention from a White House sex scandal. 9/11 has changed all that. If al-Qaeda began to rebuild what it had before, it would be bombs away—and the leaders of al-Qaeda and the Taliban know it.

My sparring partner asserts that backing away from the commitment in Afghanistan would damage U.S. credibility—a logic eerily reminiscent of the chief rationale for the war in which I served as an army officer: the one in Vietnam. The idea was as unexamined and invalid then as it is now. Governments (or terrorist groups) simply do not calculate other governments' credibility that way.[1*] Nagl's reference in this regard to how Pakistan would revisit "its recent decisions to fight against the Taliban" is odd given that the most recent decision—announced during a visit by the U.S. secretary of defense, no less—is that the Pakistani army would *not* launch any new offensives for as much as a year.

Nagl is to be commended for acknowledging that the cost of the war will be "high," and his reference to five years for building a viable Afghan government and army is more realistic than the Obama administration's timetable. The next appropriate step would be to acknowledge that the high cost in lives, limbs and money would do little or nothing to protect Americans from terrorism.

Nagl Responds

Paul Pillar argues that Afghanistan is the wrong war against the wrong enemy, that al-Qaeda has a minimal presence in Afghanistan, that victory in Afghanistan would have little effect on terrorist sanctuaries in Pakistan and elsewhere, and that the military is the wrong tool to use against our enemies.

His argument would have more force if American resources were not fungible—if the United States could not walk and chew gum at the same time. But, in fact, it is well within American means to fight a troop-intensive counterinsurgency campaign in Afghanistan, where a lack of governance and local security forces make such efforts necessary, while simultaneously pursuing a less costly form of counterinsurgency in Yemen and waging an information and education campaign against al-Qaeda in Europe and the United States. To defeat al-Qaeda the United States and its allies *must* pursue a global counterinsurgency campaign against a disaggregated enemy—using the right tools for the job in each country and region. Military power is not the right tool in every case—but it is absolutely necessary in Afghanistan.

Pillar correctly notes that depicting the struggle against al-Qaeda and the associated terror groups it inspired as a "war on terror" has overmilitarized

[1] Daryl G. Press, *Calculating Credibility: How Leaders Assess Military Threats* (Ithaca, NY: Cornell University Press, 2007).

a conflict that cannot be won through the force of arms alone. Victory in counterinsurgency comes when states afflicted by insurgents develop the independent capacity to defeat them; achieving that level of independence requires not just military training and help with killing and capturing terrorists, but also economic development and the creation of effective governance structures. In Afghanistan, in Pakistan and in many other troubled parts of the world afflicted by al-Qaeda, we focused for too long on just one aspect of this strategy.

That all changed in 2009. The United States finally began to provide the resources Afghanistan has long needed to build a stable state, and Pakistan finally began to recognize the threat that the Taliban posed to its government. More effective counterinsurgency operations on both sides of the border have put increased pressure on the Taliban and al-Qaeda; a larger Afghan army and a refocused Pakistani military are now learning to conduct counterinsurgency. It will take years and significant resources to sufficiently empower the governments and security services of both countries to stand on their own, but the investment is worth the cost.

Pillar admits that "if a terrorist group has a physical safe haven available, it will use it." There is no safe haven that al-Qaeda covets more than the border regions of Afghanistan and Pakistan, which present a unique opportunity for our enemies and a threat to us. Situated in rugged terrain hundreds of miles from any coastline, with weak or nonexistent governance and security services, this region provides both a home to al-Qaeda and possible access to nuclear weapons. Recognizing the danger, an alliance of more than forty nations is working together to clear out the terrorists, protect the population, and build the security forces and governance capacity that in time will make Afghanistan and Pakistan an unappealing base for terror.

In most places afflicted by al-Qaeda, the United States can implement counterinsurgency with a lighter footprint, providing economic-development assistance and focusing on training and equipping counterterrorism forces with local government partners. But in Afghanistan, the government and its security forces are not yet strong enough to stand on their own without significant help from us and our allies. That help is an investment in building a more secure region from which we have been brutally attacked and in which more attacks are now being planned.

Pillar is disappointed that after ousting the Taliban from power and al-Qaeda from Afghanistan, we "did not declare victory and return home." Should we do so now, we would soon have a great deal more to regret.

Paul R. Pillar is director of graduate studies at Georgetown University's Security Studies Program and a former national intelligence officer for the Near East and South Asia.

John Nagl is the president of the Center for a New American Security and a veteran of operations Desert Storm and Iraqi Freedom.

Obama Doesn't Make a Case for More Troops[*]

The Orange County Register, December 1, 2009

The leaks, orchestrated and otherwise, turned out to be not quite accurate. President Barack Obama officially took personal possession of the war in Afghanistan last night, announcing that 30,000 additional U.S. troops (not 34,000) will be hustled into Afghanistan over the next six months (not 12–18 months). He's hoping for another 10,000 or so from other NATO countries.

.The president said his first objective is not setting up the kind of counter-insurgency strategy outlined by Gen. Stanley McChrystal in his late-August memo, but active military engagement with Taliban forces with the goal of defeating or neutralizing them within 18 months, so that the U.S. can begin withdrawing U.S. troops about July 2011. Simultaneously, he anticipates a "civilian surge" that will strengthen the Afghan government's ability to deliver services and train its security forces so the Afghans can take over responsibility as quickly as possible. And he spoke of a new, closer partnership with Pakistan, where what remains of al-Qaida central is actually located.

The president acknowledged that the task will be difficult, but he didn't come close to acknowledging just how difficult it is likely to be. Afghanistan is larger and much more mountainous than Iraq, where 160,000 U.S. troops had trouble achieving control and would probably not have been able to do so, surge or no surge, if not for the Sunni Awakening, where tribal leaders abandoned al-Qaida and joined U.S. and Iraqi government forces. No such turnaround seems likely in Afghanistan, in which tribal loyalties are looser, and the population is more rural.

Perhaps most importantly, President Obama failed to make a compelling case that an escalation in Afghanistan is vital to core U.S. national interests, though he said it was several times.

All authorities acknowledge that al-Qaida, whose true strength is unknown but which has ambitions to launch new attacks on the U.S. and other Western countries, is now in the largely ungoverned tribal regions in Pakistan near the Afghan border. Nobody believes al-Qaida has a significant presence in Afghanistan. The case that it is necessary to fight in Afghanistan to neutralize al-Qaida in Pakistan is tenuous at best, and the president didn't even make the effort to strengthen it with argument and example.

The theory that an intense military effort will defeat the Taliban in Afghanistan in a year to 18 months seems more like hope than reality. The Taliban, an indigenous Afghan force, is conducting a guerrilla-style war—avoiding outright battles and preferring to strike vulnerable targets and disappear into terrain that they know much better than Americans. Typically, defeating such forces, on the rare occasions when it has been done, is a matter of years and decades rather than months and requires a government capable of winning the loyalty of the populace.

Whether it is the proper job of the United States to create a strong central government with well-trained security forces in a country that has never had, and doesn't seem to desire, such a government is another factor. The U.S. has been training Afghan forces for eight years. Can we finish the job in 18 months? It seems unlikely.

Domestically, the majority of Americans believe the Afghan war is not worth fighting, and a strong majority of his own party has serious doubts about escalation. Conservatives and Republicans are already criticizing him for not being gung ho enough, in that he stressed that this commitment is not a blank check.

The majority of Americans are correct. This war is not worth escalating.

Obama's Surge[*]

Commonweal, December 18, 2009

Did the president make a convincing case for the Afghan surge? Given the impossibility of an immediate withdrawal of U.S. forces, he made a plausible, if not always consistent or convincing, case for his plan. The United States will get in deeper—if more selectively—in order to get out more quickly. That is the pledge Obama has now made to the American people, and he should be held to it.

After three months of careful deliberation, President Barack Obama announced his strategy for bringing the eight-year-long war in Afghanistan "to a successful conclusion." Following the example of President George W. Bush's 2007 "surge" in Iraq, Obama will send more troops to Afghanistan in the hope of stabilizing a deteriorating situation and establishing conditions for the withdrawal of U.S. forces.

Did the president make a convincing case for his new strategy? Given the impossibility of an immediate withdrawal of U.S. forces, the president made a plausible, if not always consistent or convincing, case for his plan. The United States will get in deeper—if more selectively—in order to get out more quickly. That is the pledge Obama has now made to the American people, and he should be held to it.

The plan Obama put forward is at least plausible because it replicates the tactics used in the surge in Iraq, which has significantly reduced the level of violence there, thus allowing the United States to begin withdrawing its troops. Clearly Obama, once a strong opponent of the Iraq surge, has not let political rigidity keep him from embracing what he has come to understand is the best hope for relative success in Afghanistan, a war he has argued is necessary. What is not wholly convincing about Obama's plan, however, is how it deals with the fact that Afghanistan—a desperately poor, largely rural, and preliterate country—is even less amenable to U.S. intervention than

Iraq. Much will depend on how well the policy is executed and how strongly it is supported by NATO and other allies. Even more will depend on the cooperation and reliability of our often corrupt Afghan allies and the often reluctant Pakistanis. The president's new strategy remains a big gamble, but it is difficult to argue that his decision is a self-serving one, especially given the opposition of many within his own party.

Where Obama's surge differs significantly from President Bush's is in his determination to set a date, July 2011, to begin drawing down U.S. forces. Setting a deadline, Obama insists, is necessary to provide a "sense of urgency in working with the Afghan government." Although the president has in essence taken the advice of his generals, he has also made it clear that his commitment to the military's counterinsurgency strategy is not open-ended. He wants results and he wants them quickly, and if the strategy fails he is willing to move in a different direction.

"I refuse to set goals that go beyond our responsibility, our means, or our interests," he told the nation in his West Point speech announcing his decision. Eschewing any triumphalism, the speech was remarkably somber in its tone and detailed in its arguments. "America will have to show our strength in the way that we end wars and prevent conflict—not just how we wage wars," he cautioned. In an effort to summon a sense of national unity—a unity squandered by the decision to invade Iraq—the president even tried to answer honest objections to his decision. Many skeptics argue that the threat posed by Al Qaeda is no longer located in Afghanistan, but in Pakistan and elsewhere, and thus the resurgence of the Afghan Taliban does not pose an imminent danger to the United States. Obama insisted, however, that a return of the Taliban to power in Afghanistan would embolden Al Qaeda and possibly destabilize Pakistan. It is in our vital national-security interest to "break the momentum" of that resurgence, something that cannot be done "from a distance." Obama further insisted that his new strategy, with its emphasis on protecting population centers and a willingness to enlist local Afghan leaders, including some Taliban, will provide Afghanistan's warring factions enough breathing room to broker a modus vivendi. For that to work, Pakistan must further intensify its efforts to root out the Taliban and what remains of Al Qaeda in the border regions.

There are few good options available to the president, but it is hard to believe that security conditions in Afghanistan can be dramatically improved in eighteen months. As the precarious stability of Iraq reminds us, insurgencies require political, not merely military, solutions. Does the United States have the diplomatic skills—and the diplomatic partners—to make that happen? After eight years of intermittent engagement, there is little evidence we do.

'The West Can Encourage Legitimacy and Accountability'*

By Aziz Hakimi
Boston Review, January/February 2010

Nir Rosen argues that the U.S. military strategy in Afghanistan is likely to fail and that the Karzai government is irredeemably illegitimate. I agree with the first point, but not with the second.

The United States, as Rosen says, has used a narrowly military lens in formulating its strategy. While recognizing that a military solution is insufficient for addressing the conflict, the United States has decided to escalate troop deployment. This course of action has been tried, and it has failed.

When the problem is cast in combat terms—Afghanistan as a theater in the "war on terrorism"—the solutions are inevitably military. But the central problem in Afghanistan is political. Past failures to achieve a political settlement have prolonged the war and created an internal war, a civil war between ethnic and regional groupings vying for power. Even the Karzai government, which has always been presented as a government of national unity and has included all the Afghan factions except the Taliban, is now party to the conflict. Political settlement and national reconciliation are the only solutions that will work.

I disagree with Rosen, however, that Afghanistan's government—especially since August's fraudulent election—is hopelessly illegitimate and cannot be reformed.

Part of the problem may be that Western policymakers have the wrong idea about what constitutes a "strong" state. Afghanistan does not need a centralized state with a massive military and police presence. This will only fuel the unrest. Instead it needs a loosening of the centralized state. Afghanistan's future lies in devolving power to the local level; developing a consensual politics that meets the aspirations of all its peoples; and instituting a non-intrusive, but effective, state that empowers people in their cities and villages while reducing the authority of the elites and powerbrokers in Kabul, who often use their influence in pursuit of personal gain and political loyalty. Rosen is correct when he says that the Americans "[overemphasize] the importance of tribalism in Afghan society." The real problem lies in the Afghan state's historical approach to rural communities: a policy of divide-and-rule by the Pashtun-dominated ruling class.

It is also tempting to assume that corruption is endemic to Afghanistan. The corruption is, indeed, terrible, but the United States and its allies share some blame. The warlords that President Obama wants thrown out of government were brought to power by his predecessor and remain useful to U.S. and allied forces. Like the West, Karzai has no ideological alliance with them. Instead, he lacks broad popular support, so he relies on existing influential figures, many tainted by allegations of human rights violations, abuse of power, and criminal activity.

But just as the West bolstered a corrupt regime, so too can it encourage legitimacy and accountability. President Karzai must be given incentives to reduce his dependence on warlords and drug traffickers. Demonizing and isolating him will force him to seek alternative sources of support, which is precisely what happened after the West started criticizing him and his government.

And a new Western strategy in Afghanistan must include a partnership not just with Karzai's government, but also with the Afghan people, and focus consistently and patiently on long-term political solutions. Such a strategy would have four elements:

First, a genuine dialogue with relevant, non-executive forces in Afghan society, including the parliament, civil society organizations, and the armed opposition. A lasting peace will require reconciliation among Afghanistan's warring factions: the government; former jihadi leaders; and the many insurgent groups, particularly the Taliban. Obama is correct in his assessment that the "war in Afghanistan cannot be won without convincing non-ideologically committed insurgents to lay down their arms, reject al Qaeda, and accept the Afghan Constitution."

When development aid is linked to military objectives and aims to buy Afghan 'hearts and minds,' it becomes an easy target for the Taliban.

Yet, while some efforts have been made to make contact and hold negotiations with insurgent groups, a credible road map for reconciliation has not been worked out. The United States has unhelpfully rejected negotiations with "Mullah Omar and the Taliban's hard core that have aligned themselves with al Qaeda," and factionalism has prevented the Afghan government from taking the less ideological approach that might bring the Taliban into the fold. To move forward, the United States and its allies must be more pragmatic. The Taliban must be allowed to enter the political mainstream. Furthermore, the U.S. role should be to facilitate—not dictate—a genuine reconciliation among Afghans. The legitimacy of the Afghan government would be greatly strengthened if it led the process.

Second, Afghanistan's dysfunctional state requires reform. Legitimacy is enhanced through the provision of basic services, including security, but also depends on the government's identity and the inclusiveness of political institutions. In tandem with reconciliation efforts, then, are measures to devolve state power and resources out of Kabul. After eight years of limited success in rebuilding Afghanistan's political and economic infrastructure, international donors must persuade the Afghan government to decentralize. Instead of simply blaming President Karzai for his failures or threatening to deal directly with subnational actors, influential outsiders should encourage consensus on this reform. With greater authority in the hands of local leaders, individual Afghans will be better disposed to their leaders at all levels and have greater say in the administrative matters that affect them.

Devolving political power to the village, district, and provincial levels raises difficult issues of local accountability, and doing so may bring the "bad guys" into the political arena, necessitating additional reform efforts later. But Afghanistan's problems cannot be solved at once. They will have to be tackled gradually.

Third, the Afghan people must have the authority and capability to reconstruct and develop their lives and livelihoods. When development aid is linked to military objectives and aims to buy Afghan "hearts and minds" with deliveries from the American military and private contractors, it becomes an easy target for the Taliban. Much more promising is capital investment in those communities, institutions, and programs that have proven responsive to popular needs. At the same time, transparency mechanisms should be fully utilized in order to reduce corruption.

Fourth, a new strategy must spur cooperation among Afghan civil society groups, which currently are isolated and weak and compete with each other for foreign funds. There are hundreds of Afghan-led successes across the country; however, the Afghan people are generally unaware of them. Indeed, foreign donors have made every effort to take the credit. If these activities are seen as indigenous Afghan building blocks, which they are, their success will continue, and they will draw more Afghans away from the insurgency.

Long-term peace in Afghanistan is possible. In the past, military force brought short-term stability—the Taliban in the second half of the 1990s and the U.S.-led intervention in November 2001. Both partially succeeded because the Afghan people were tired of war and ready to try the alternative. But long-term peace can only be accomplished with a political solution that includes national reconciliation, privileges ownership and control by local actors, and encourages cooperation among the Afghan civil society groups that can hold the government to account.

The Slog of War[*]

By Nir Rosen
Mother Jones, January/February 2010

Major Jim Contreras was awaiting his marching orders. Literally. Stuck in Lashkar Gah, the capital of the Afghan province of Helmand, he was supposed to take his troops, along with a unit of an elite Afghan police force known as ANCOP, to secure the area around Nawa, so the people there could vote. It was part of the past year's biggest US offensive against the Taliban. But he couldn't leave, because his Afghan counterparts hadn't gotten their official order from the Ministry of Interior. The order had been signed five days earlier, but it had to be delivered to the commander, Colonel Gulam Sakhi Gahfori, by courier, with its seal intact. Then again, Colonel Sakhi had also not gotten basic supplies like fuel, ammunition, and radios. Contreras and Sakhi spent a fair amount of time discussing how the Afghans were to refuel at Nawa. Nobody knew if there were any gas stations there.

Contreras is a small man with a big grin who served in Bosnia, Haiti, and the first Gulf War. He was excited about his work in Afghanistan. He believed he was fighting to protect the American way of life. His wife had been working near the Pentagon when it was hit on 9/11. "This is in its infancy," he said. "We're beginning to see the military might that we as a nation can bring."

That evening Contreras' men, an Illinois National Guard unit dubbed Team Ironhorse, sat waiting to be briefed by their CO. The dozen men were all scouts, and some were snipers, all trained by their recently killed first lieutenant to be "meat eaters." But the months of daily operations and [defecating] in bags had taken a toll. They resented being sent on missions that weren't theirs, the neglect they felt, the lack of progress. One sergeant's parents owned a hardware store and sent the team four tow straps to pull their vehicles out of sand and mud because their request through military channels had gone nowhere.

Major Contreras said Ironhorse's mission was to escort the ANCOP to the Nawa area, which a Marine unit was trying to secure so Afghan authorities could take over. He also said guys in police uniforms were harassing civilians. Whether they were impostors or Afghan National Police (ANP)—the ordinary and often corrupt cops that Ironhorse's ANCOP partners looked down on—was anyone's guess. He told his men to plan for seven days in the field. "The reason why we're going down is to put an Afghan face on the mission," he said.

The men looked skeptical. "Duration of mission and number of legitimate police in Nawa and how will ANP get along with ANCOP?" Staff Sergeant Robert McGuire tersely asked without moving or looking at the major. Staff Sergeant Tim Verdoorn complained that Team Ironhorse would be doing the Marines' job. As the major concluded his briefing, McGuire loudly muttered, "It's a [bad situation]." After Contreras left, McGuire added, "That was very well thought out." I asked him to elaborate. "Fuel will be the biggest issue," he said. "We don't know where we're gonna live. We're not taking tents."

Contreras had his own worries. The Marines had chosen a school as their base, and British forces in the area had warned against occupying schools. "The Marines are trained to go off a ship, hit the ground, and [really] charge," he told me later. They might not be suited for counterinsurgency.

Counterinsurgency, or COIN, has been in vogue at the Pentagon since the success of the Iraq surge, and its dominance was cemented when President Obama chose General Stanley McChrystal, former head of special operations forces and a recent convert to counterinsurgency, as his commander in Afghanistan. Shortly afterward, Obama promulgated his new strategy "to disrupt, dismantle, and defeat Al Qaeda in Pakistan and Afghanistan." The primary tool would be COIN.

Counterinsurgency theorists obsessively study "small wars," such as the British war in Malaya, the French war in Algeria, and the wars in Vietnam. The emphasis is on using the least amount of violence against the enemy, familiarity with the local culture, and painstakingly removing popular support for the insurgents. This involves using proxy forces to kill those who cannot be "reconciled," and searching for political solutions that tempt the civilian population away from the insurgents.

In some ways, COIN and the related "stability operations" doctrine are a rejection of the neoconservative focus on military might as the key tool of foreign policy. Just as the neocons ruled the Pentagon under George W. Bush, so it seems that the proponents of "population-centric" fighting now have a preponderance of influence in the Obama administration.

To liberals, these COINdinistas, as they are dubbed, might seem kindred spirits. They emphasize nonlethal means, humanitarian aid, development work, and protecting the civilian population. They recognize that military force alone cannot solve conflicts, and that in Iraq and Afghanistan, the US military did not know how to operate in a war where "the terrain is the people." But the end result is still a foreign military occupation—which is not America's stated goal in Afghanistan.

Contreras and I drove to Sakhi's office at the ANCOP headquarters (the acronym stands for Afghan National Civil Order Police). There was a marijuana plant in the garden, and inside a picture of President Hamid Karzai was flanked by some plastic flowers and a map of Helmand. Sakhi was wearing an ornate shalwar kameez, cream with shiny embroidery, and watching a Bollywood movie. He had thick eyebrows and a short, well-groomed beard. He brought out a pile of kebab and bread and bantered with his guests through Bariyal, a thickly muscled translator known as Shotgun. He was the 2002 weight-lifting champion in Pakistan's North West Frontier Province, and like most translators who spend enough time with the Americans, he had adopted their argot. "ANCOP are [very] badass people," he told me. Colonel Sakhi and Team Ironhorse shared the same warrior culture, and the language divide proved easily surmountable.

Sakhi strongly believed that most Taliban were locals, working on farms, firing when they had a chance, then throwing down their weapons and taking up a shovel. He warned that the Taliban had planted at least 100 IEDS in Nawa. IEDs had been responsible for the majority of American and British casualties in Afghanistan and a few months before had claimed Team Ironhorse's lieutenant and a staff sergeant, as well as an interpreter and an ANCOP officer. It happened last February when First Lieutenant Jared Southworth and Staff Sergeant Jason Burkholder went to examine an IED the ANCOP had discovered. They asked for an ordnance disposal team to destroy it because they worried civilians would get blown up, but were told to mark the location and move on. The ANCOP officer dismantled the IED anyway, but a second one beneath blew up. Ironhorse spent an hour picking pieces of their friends off the road and out of a tree.

First Lieutenant Southworth had been very passionate, his men told me. He believed he'd come to give Afghan kids a better future and he loved what he was doing. He paid Afghans $150 for pointing out IEDs. A rich aunt sent him the money. It was unusual but it worked, his men said. Back in Illinois, they had been told they would be on a large base in a safe job, but Southworth knew different. He informed them they were going into the s**t. He spent more than a year preparing the team as best he could, sending them to sniper school, scout school, combat lifesaver school, mountain warfare school. He gave a speech to the men just prior to deployment, warning that some of them wouldn't make it back.

Mindful of IEDs, Contreras told Sakhi that Ironhorse would go through the desert to avoid the main road. The Marines would meet them to guide them to the schoolhouse base. But Sakhi had still not received his written orders. He asked Contreras to tell the American police-training headquarters in Kandahar to email the deputy minister of interior. The next day Contreras went to see Sakhi again. "The Marines are giving me a lot of problems because of the delay," he said. Sakhi was still waiting for supplies. One of the major operations of the year, the military's big push to ensure Afghanistan could hold its election, was being held up by red tape.

Two days later they finally got the order to go. Sergeant McGuire was in command of the lead National Guard Humvee. The gunner up top shot pen flares that went *pop* like a gun at cars that got too close. McGuire asked if I was sure I wanted to be in the first vehicle, which would be the first one to get blown up by IEDS. Sakhi asked that the Americans' armored vehicles take the lead because his vehicles would be blown to shreds.

As we drove south the ANCOP stopped in front of every culvert to search both sides. It was slow progress. Some of the police trucks got stuck in the deep, soft sand. When we reached the Arghandab River, the ANCOP drivers started playing NASCAR, speeding around each other, nearly crashing. Two of them got into an argument about the driving and one raised his rifle. This had happened before, Sergeant Verdoom later told me. Once, on the base, two of the ANCOP had drawn their pistols on each other. "There was blood in their eyes," Verdoom said.

Two Marine Humvees met Ironhorse across the river. We were in a thickly vegetated area of farmland, trees, and narrow canals. Helmand is the wealthiest province in Afghanistan; it has an irrigation system, some electricity and paved roads, and some of the best agricultural land in the region. It is the world's largest producer of opium poppies and a great place for a self-sustaining insurgency.

Sandbags lined the top of the schoolhouse. Hundreds of Marines wandered around shirtless wearing green shorts and kicking up dust. They slept on the ground outside or in classrooms that smelled of sweaty feet. A Marine captain thanked Contreras for bringing the ANCOP. The lack of an Afghan face had been their weak spot, he said. Nawa had been quiet for a few days. "The Taliban left to lie low," he said, "but this is their breadbasket, so they're not likely to give it up."

The next morning Contreras met Marine Commander William McCollough at Patrol Base Jaker, a partially constructed brick building that was a short but tense walk from the schoolhouse. McCollough told Contreras that in the town of Aynak, 14 miles away, they had discovered a "rogue" police unit that was extorting the locals. Nawa's chief of police, Nafas Khan, sat in on the meeting. He had a long beard and a long, nervous face. The Marines described him as a local mafia boss. Team Ironhorse suspected he was keeping his men's salary for himself, forcing the police to steal for a living. Khan denied that the police in Aynak were under his authority.

After Khan left, McCollough told Sakhi that he should supplant the rogue police. The Marines might have to fight to get to Aynak, but once there, McCollough said, they would meet with locals in a *shura*, or council. Team Ironhorse's Staff Sergeant Randy Thacker was dismissive. "These shuras are just a bitch session," he said. "They'll complain about cops shaking them down.

The major will make promises and the ANP will come back and go back to the same ways." He'd seen it before: When Ironhorse and the ANCOP came in, towns that had been abandoned would slowly repopulate, and when they started to hand things back over to the ANP, residents would flee once more. The ANP were the only face of the Afghan government most people saw, and it was often an ugly one.

The three units prepared for departure the following morning. The Marines gave Ironhorse and ANCOP enough fuel for another day or so. What might happen after that, no one really knew.

The next day the coalition command for Helmand informed Contreras that the Aynak police were indeed under Khan's authority. We departed at 5 a.m. and rumbled slowly along a canal green with vegetation. Marine minesweepers walked ahead of us. By 9 a.m., we had gone maybe three miles—a numbing pace that allowed any Taliban to flee well in advance.

Children tended cows and sheep in fields. At 10:30 we linked up with a group of Marines who would take us the rest of the way to Aynak. Dozens of their vehicles were parked off the dirt road on plowed fields, crushing cornstalks. "This farmer is not gonna be happy," one corporal said. The Marines had paid damages to farmers in the area. Today they accidentally set one field on fire, then ran around trying to put it out. The shura in Aynak was canceled because it was clear we would be getting there too late. Marines lay about in the shade. A young specialist sat atop a Humvee. "We came, we parked, we relocated, then we parked," he beamed.

A Marine captain named Andrew Schoenmaker arrived and told Contreras that when his men had first asked people in Aynak about the Taliban, they got only complaints about the police. He estimated that there were about 150 cops. "It was uncomfortable when we met them," he said. "They were all high."

We wouldn't be leaving for Aynak until 4:30 in the afternoon. That concerned Sergeant Verdoorn: "It seems like the Marines want to get in a firefight—5:30 p.m. is the beginning of fighting time." I asked Contreras about the delay and he said, "Because it is [very] hot." The Marines had to walk, and in the past few days dozens of them had collapsed from heat exhaustion.

We finally began to plod along once more, the Marines in front of us. Kids stood motionless in front of homes and glared at the Americans. Men with black beards and black turbans also stared, expressionless, standing ramrod straight.

A boy emerged from behind a metal gate and mud walls to talk to the ANCOP, but none of them spoke Pashto and he didn't know Farsi. The Americans' interpreter translated. There was an IED on the road up ahead, the boy said. His father came out wearing a green shalwar kameez and nervously fingering red prayer beads. The IED was planted near their house. Several days before, Taliban had been hiding in a house about a few hundred feet away, he said, pointing to it. He worried locals would inform the Taliban that they had warned the Americans. McGuire walked right up to the IED and saw it partially buried and concealed by shrubs. The minesweepers ahead of us had missed it. A robot was dispatched to destroy it; the explosion sent up a huge cloud of smoke and debris. Rocks rained down on us hundreds of feet away. The men speculated whether it would have been a catastrophic kill. McGuire thought it would have just tossed us up a bit in our armored vehicle. But it would have obliterated the ANCOP.

We made it to Aynak after nightfall. It had taken an entire day to go 14 miles. We slept under the stars, the men taking turns on guard shift. We heard explosions and gunfire in the distance. The next morning the police used an abandoned mud compound as a bathroom, and so did I.

Colonel Shirzad, the AP commander for Helmand, showed up. Like every other chief of police in Helmand, he had bought his post from officials at the Ministry of Interior. Police were known to release prisoners for bribes ranging from $500 to $15,000. I hitched a ride back to Lashkar Gah with Shirzad, sitting in one of the four Ford Rangers in his convoy. It took us 30 minutes. The trip from Lashkar Gah to Aynak had taken Ironhorse three days. Shirzad's men did not stop to check for IEDS, which could shred their Rangers. I scanned the road desperately.

The next morning, I learned, Ironhorse went out on patrol with the AN-COP and found five IEDS placed on the road I had just taken. One had been hidden by their invisible adversary just after they had passed; they found it on the return trip. That day a 20-vehicle Marine convoy from a base in the desert tried to go to Aynak to resupply Ironhorse. The convoy was attacked by the Taliban so fiercely that it turned back.

Colonel Bill Hix is an experienced Special Forces officer with extensive COIN experience who until July led the Afghan Regional Security Integration Command in Kandahar—he was in charge of training and mentoring the Afghan police and army. I met him there just before he shipped home. His wall featured portraits of 41 Americans from his command who had been killed, all but 2 by IEDS. He would have needed a much bigger wall for the Afghans. From January 2007 to April of 2009, he had lost 2,096 Afghan police and 949 Afghan army soldiers.

Hix believed that the Taliban's disappearance in the face of an American operation was a sign not of weakness, but of strategy. They would slide their Kalashnikovs under their beds and bide their time, watching their enemy. It had happened with a major operation in another part of Helmand the year before; as soon as the Americans left, the Taliban were back. Hix had spent 21 months in Afghanistan, and he enjoyed his job. In his view it was the Afghan army's job to push the Taliban away from the population, while the police should be protecting the people where they lived. Hix did not believe more American troops were needed, just an "adequate" police force and army—about double the present number, which had taken eight years to build up.

Control is essential to a successful counterinsurgency campaign. According to Stathis Kalyvas, the Yale political scientist and civil war expert whose book *The Logic of Violence in Civil War* is very influential among counterinsurgency theorists, "The higher the level of control exercised by the actor, the higher the rate of collaboration with this actor—and, inversely, the lower the rate of defection." But by that logic, the Americans will never have enough troops in Afghanistan to achieve control. A generally accepted ratio for a successful counterinsurgency is roughly 1 cop or soldier per 50 civilians. That would mean 600,000 troops are needed to secure Afghanistan—fewer if part of the country is assumed to be secure already. The Afghan army and police between them have about 189,000 members, and there are an additional 42,000 international (mostly NATO) troops in the country. Obama has raised the US total in Afghanistan from 47,000 to 68,000. McChrystal's much-debated request is for an additional 40,000, but even that would bring the US troop total in Afghanistan to about 68 percent of the number in Iraq, a smaller country, at the peak of the surge.

Meanwhile the Taliban are seamlessly embedded within communities, a British security expert in Helmand told me. They *are* the locals. They do not need Kalashnikovs; a simple knock on the door can be just as effective. At night the Taliban controls the villages, undoing whatever the Americans tried to accomplish during the day. It does not matter if here and there the Americans are effective. "Emptying out the *Titanic* with a teacup has an effect," the Brit told me, "but it doesn't stop the ship from sinking."

COIN is a massive endeavor, I was told by retired Colonel Patrick Lang, who has done counterinsurgency in Vietnam, Latin America, and the Middle East. There are insufficient resources committed to doing it in Afghanistan, he says, and if the Americans don't plan on owning the country, why waste time on it? "It is only worth the expenditure of resources if you were the local government seeking to establish authority, or an imperialist power that wanted to hang around for a while." There are 28 million people in Afghanistan, and they are widely dispersed in small towns. "You have to provide security for the whole country," Lang told me, "because if you move around they just move in behind you and undo what you did. So you need to have effective security and a massive multifaceted development organization that covers the whole place. COIN advisers have to stay in place all the time. If you're going to do COIN, it really amounts to nation building, and troops are there to provide protection for the nation builders."

His point was that the Americans will bail on Afghanistan no matter what. It will be tragic when that happens, whether it's six months from now or two years from now. Andrew Wilder, a longtime aid worker who has spent years working in Afghanistan and set up its first think tank, the Afghanistan Research and Evaluation Unit, told me there is no way to "fix" Afghanistan. "It may be more realistic to look for ways to slow down the descent into anarchy." Another way to look at it came from a retired American military officer working in security in Afghanistan. "Every time our boys face them, we win," he told me grimly. "We're winning every day. Are we going to keep winning for 20 years?"

3

Iraq: Should We Stay or Should We Go?

Editor's Introduction

Until recently, the issue of whether the United States should significantly reduce its military presence in Iraq seemed settled. In February 2009, President Obama announced that all combat troops would return home by August 31, 2010, leaving the country in the hands of the Iraqi military and a U.S. "transitional force," there mostly to provide support, that would withdraw by 2011. However, in February 2010, reports surfaced that military officials were considering keeping troops in Iraq beyond the stated deadline. During national elections held in March, Iraqi Prime Minister Nouri al-Maliki indicated that he might ask U.S. forces to stay put and help stabilize the country, depending "on whether the established Iraqi army and police would be enough" to do the job themselves.

Talk of prolonged troop deployment sparked renewed debate over the then-seven-year-old war, a conflict that had, for a time, disappeared from the headlines and ceased to be a major political issue. In the wake of President Bush's 2007 troop surge, violence seemed to be on the wane, and during the first three months of 2010, there was only one U.S. combat fatality. Afghanistan had suddenly become the hot-button war, and many Americans figured the Iraq conundrum was finally headed toward some kind of resolution.

The selections in this chapter look ahead to Iraq's uncertain future, considering what role the United States should play in supporting the country's fledgling democracy. In "How Deep In After We're Out?" the first entry, Frank Oliveri considers whether the twin threats of factional violence and increased interference from Iran are sufficient reasons to remain in Iraq. Lawmakers are split: while Republican senator John McCain of Arizona says he supports staying in Iraq, so long as casualty rates remain low, Democratic congressman David R. Obey of Wisconsin insists it's time to leave. "In the long term, that region is much better with us out," he tells Oliveri.

In "Extending Our Stay in Iraq," the next piece in this chapter, Thomas E. Ricks paints a gloomy picture of Iraq, writing, "The political situation is far less certain, and I think less stable, than most Americans believe." Withdrawing troops prematurely would be tantamount to "rushing toward failure," he adds, stoking fears that an Iraq without U.S. troops is sure to devolve into chaos. He advocates keeping 30,000 to 50,000 troops on the ground to prevent an all-out civil war. Jeremy R. Hammond refutes Ricks' points in the next article, "The Rationale for Keeping U.S. Forces in Iraq," questioning whether a civil war is truly on the horizon.

Tom Engelhardt doesn't disagree that Iraq could be heading for disaster, but in the subsequent piece, "Doomsday in Iraq—Is It Really Just Around the Corner?" he contends that such a fear is no reason to keep troops there past the deadline. "It's true that terrible things may happen in Iraq," he writes. "They could happen while we are there. They could happen with us gone. But history delivers its surprises more regularly than we imagine—even in Iraq."

In the following entry, "Hope and Change in Iraq," Reuel Marc Gerecht takes an optimistic look at the country's political landscape, envisioning an Iraq in which Sunni and Shiite Muslims live in peace. Gerecht writes that the United States should maintain a troop presence in Iraq—not to intervene in elections or "choose sides" between warring factions, but rather to play a support role, as it did in Europe after World War II. He feels "a constructive, unobtrusive U.S. presence is doable," past mistakes notwithstanding.

The next article, "Long Goodbye, but Goodbye," finds the editors of the *Palm Beach Post* making the case for sticking with the 2011 withdrawal deadline. The authors call the war "distracting," "tragic," and "expensive," blaming President Bush for using bad intelligence and, in their view, outright lies to start a war that they believe never should have been fought. In the final piece, "Rebirth of a Nation," Babak Dehghanpisheh, John Barry, and Christopher Dickey examine what U.S. Army general David Petraeus has called "Iraqracy," the nascent form of democracy that has taken hold in Iraq. The authors acknowledge there are many challenges still facing the Middle Eastern nation, but they also predict it will become a regional power, signaling what they term a "dark victory" for the United States.

How Deep in After We're Out?[*]

By Frank Oliveri
Congressional Quarterly Weekly, March 13, 2010

When fewer than 40 people were killed on Election Day in Iraq last week, it was one reason the national vote was hailed as a success. More important, turnout was strong, at 62 percent, and the initial results were seen as a relative vote of confidence in Iraqi Prime Minister Nouri al-Maliki.

It will probably still take months for Iraqi leaders to form a new coalition government. But officials in the United States, who have long said a successful election would allow American troops to accelerate their departure, are already breathing a sigh of relief. Indeed, the downsizing of the U.S. force is proceeding ahead of schedule. Currently at 96,000, the number should be down to 50,000 by the end of August.

In hailing Iraq's election, President Obama last week repeated his pledge that "by the end of next year, all U.S. troops will be out of Iraq." Such a withdrawal would mark a politically important milestone for the president, who won the White House partly on his pledge to end one of the most divisive wars in the nation's history—a conflict that will mark its seventh anniversary this coming weekend.

Yet few U.S. or Iraqi officials genuinely expect all of the soldiers and Marines to be gone from the country after December 2011. For one thing, many of the political and security problems that plagued Iraq before the Bush administration's 2007 troop surge remain unresolved. Beyond that, many American and Iraqi government officials see a U.S. presence, however diminished, as a bulwark against continued sectarian factionalism and Iranian efforts to exert influence over the government and the region.

Indeed, negotiations between the two governments are already under way to determine the shape of future U.S.-Iraqi relations, which will probably include some American military presence in Iraq for the foreseeable future.

* Reprinted with permission of Congressional Quarterly Inc., from CQ *Weekly*, article byFrank Oliveri, March 13, 2010, Vol. 68 Issue 11. © 2010; permission conveyed through Copyright Clearance Center, Inc.

Whatever shape that force takes, the Obama administration and Congress will face some fundamental decisions regarding the number of troops staying behind and what their mission will be—not to mention how to manage the expectations of the public, in both countries, that the United States would be getting out of Iraq completely.

"As we continue to live up to our commitments under the security agreement, it has actually increased our credibility in Iraq as an honest broker," Colin Kahl, the deputy assistant secretary of Defense for the Middle East, said at a recent conference on Iraq. "You see the Iraqis asking for our help, not just for us to provide initiatives, but to help facilitate their initiatives and help identify solutions that are based on their initiatives."

Maliki echoed this view in a CNN interview during his country's voting, saying he might ask U.S. forces to remain beyond the deadline depending "on whether the established Iraqi army and police would be enough or not."

Brent Scowcroft, who was the national security adviser from 1989 to 1993 for President George Bush, said that while Iraq's commitment to ending the U.S. military involvement in 2011 initially seemed "concrete," the country's leaders now appear to be "hedging." As a consequence, "we ought to adapt a more flexible state of mind," he said. "We ought to be more flexible about when we leave, and the manner in which we leave."

The new Iraqi government will largely determine the contours of any future relationship. "It's not our call," said Kahl, who is the Pentagon's top Iraq policy official. But Maliki's willingness to consider a longer-lasting U.S. military presence underscores the acknowledgement, even in Baghdad, that Iraqis have a long way to go before they can stand on their own.

The U.S. military has clearly become a stabilizing presence in Iraq in the past year. But as the number of U.S. troops gets smaller, the risks to stability get bigger. Iraqis still have to confront ethnic and sectarian divisions—few more important than Arab-Kurd relations in the north, where there are disputes over who controls the oil-rich city of Kirkuk. And the government in Baghdad is committed to taking on greater responsibility for internal security and other services, as well as modernizing the military to guard against external threats. "Clearly, the ball is in the court of the Iraqi government," said Sen. Jack Reed of Rhode Island, a senior Democrat on the Armed Services Committee.

But Iraq will still be dependent on the U.S. military for some central functions, including logistics and intelligence operations. If the government's modernization efforts lag or sectarian violence re-emerges, prompting a formal request from Baghdad for a sizable U.S. force to remain beyond 2011, Iraq could vault back toward the top of the congressional agenda just as the nation's political attention turns to Obama's presumed campaign for a second term and the Republican primaries to select his opponent. With a remarkably low U.S. casualty rate—just a single combat death in the past three months—the once divisive Iraq issue has nearly disappeared from the U.S. political arena. Still, the House spent three hours last week debating a resolution calling for a withdrawal from Afghanistan that, while overwhelmingly defeated, was a reminder that the politics of war are never far from the Capitol.

To be sure, there are those who say it is possible Iraq will decide not to seek a U.S. military presence. Ike Skelton, the Missouri Democrat who chairs the House Armed Services Committee, said, "I can honestly see a new government just saying let's not rewrite" the status of forces agreement, which sets the parameters for the American military involvement.

Either way, as the administration is quick to point out, the United States plans to remain involved in shaping the future of Iraq no matter what happens with the troops. The State Department is taking on an increasing role in supporting the Iraqi government, including providing localized aid and expertise, as well as training a robust internal Iraqi police force. "The withdrawal of our forces from Iraq is not about disengagement," Kahl said. "In fact, our engagement with Iraq will increase." He added, "We want it. The Iraqis want it."

A NEW MISSION

To reduce the force to 50,000 by next summer, the Pentagon will have to embark on one of the most ambitious logistical operations in its history, bringing home many of the 2.58 million pieces of equipment left after more than seven years of war and occupation. Even then, as much as 30 percent of the gear will be left behind—from trucks and radar dishes to flat-screen televisions and desktop computers—because it's been judged too worn down or too costly to ship. The Pentagon already has Congress' blessing to give up to $750 million worth of equipment to Iraq.

Once the force is at 50,000, the military's role will shift fundamentally away from combat and toward training, advice and assistance. The U.S. wants to develop the Iraqi military to the point where it could plausibly fill the vacuum created by the American drawdown. To that end, U.S. forces would have three main missions from September 2010 to December 2011: Protecting civilian workers for federal agencies and the United Nations, helping the Iraqi military, and engaging in counterterrorism operations to keep pressure on Al Qaeda in Iraq. Underlying these tasks are ongoing efforts, begun eight months ago, to shift responsibilities from the U.S. military to either the Iraqi government or to U.S. civilian agencies.

The half-dozen or so brigades remaining beyond August will be formally termed "advise and assist" forces, but they are essentially combat units equipped with significant firepower. They will be accompanied by specially trained advisers, with language skills and cultural know-how to help them hone Iraqi commanders' abilities to command and control their forces.

The generals will also make sure they retain sufficient muscle to protect U.S. bases, diplomatic posts and civilian agency operations. Analysts and lawmakers expect that some units could be used for counterterrorism operations, to provide a buffer between rival Iraq factions or even to step in if Iraqi forces are overwhelmed. In other words, while the force would be significantly smaller, it would still be among the most formidable in the region. "We won't be the most numerous army in Iraq," said the Pentagon's Kahl, but "we will be a pretty capable force."

A big part of the new mission will be transforming the Iraqi military from one of the most robust counterinsurgency forces in the Middle East into one capable of defending the nation's borders.

Doing so is expected to take several years because it entails modernizing the entire Iraqi military, including integrating U.S.-built tanks and aircraft. The Iraqi Air Force, for example, currently consists of only a smattering of helicopters, transport planes and training aircraft. But Iraq is looking to buy hundreds of fighter jets, including American-made F-16s.

Just that extensive outfitting of the Iraqi military leads many to predict with confidence that U.S. forces will remain well beyond 2011. "Every Iraqi senior leader I have spoken to over the last several months agrees that some U.S. force will be needed," said retired Army Lt. Gen. James M. Dubik, a senior fellow at the Institute for the Study of War, who oversaw the training of Iraqi security forces in 2007 and 2008.

"They've committed to M1A1 tanks," adds Gen. Ray Odierno of the Army, the top commander in Iraq. "They've committed to helicopters. These will go beyond 2011, so there'll be some requirement for us to continue to coordinate and help them to bring those systems onboard."

TO WITHDRAW OR NOT TO WITHDRAW

How an Iraqi request for U.S. forces to remain beyond 2011 would fare in Congress would depend mightily on whether troops were still dying there. "The context for that decision is important," said Senate Foreign Relations Chairman John Kerry, a Massachusetts Democrat.

Senators of both parties on the Armed Services Committee echoed that concern. Missouri Democrat Claire McCaskill said she would want to know how large the proposed force would be and what its mission would be beyond training. The chairman, Michigan Democrat Carl Levin, and Virginia Democrat Jim Webb noted that the existing agreements with Iraq give the United States flexibility for leaving a force of some size behind.

"We've always contemplated a small number of troops for anti-terror; that has always been on the table," Levin said, adding that forces to protect the embassy, and to provide training for a multinational U.N. presence, would not give him pause.

But such provisions make other lawmakers uneasy. "I'm concerned that in the end there's going to be tremendous pressure for us not to maintain our scheduled withdrawal from Iraq," Wisconsin Democrat David R. Obey, chairman of the House Appropriations Committee, said in a hearing last month.

Webb, too, is worried that keeping U.S. troops in Iraq is against U.S. interests. "In the long term, that region is much better with us out," he said. "We need to leave Iraq in a timely manner."

Some analysts have suggested that to keep Iraq stable beyond 2012 as many as 35,000 troops will need to remain. Publicly, many Democrats reject that notion; Levin, for example, says what he's got in mind would involve a force of only a few hundred. He and Webb are both of the view that it will take a near-total drawdown to compel Iraqi leaders to confront and overcome their internal political discord.

Some Democratic liberals have a more black-or-white view. Arizona's Raul M. Grijalva, who co-chairs the House Progressive Caucus, says his group would launch a legislative effort to prevent any long-term U.S. military presence in Iraq.

Another obstacle could be the price tag. Obey recently estimated the annual cost of keeping 40,000 troops in or near Iraq at about $25 billion—a figure that anti-war liberals will seize on as untenable at a time of economic anxiety and high deficits. Iraq, said Democratic Rep. Dennis J. Kucinich of Ohio, is already "draining this country's ability to take care of its own."

Defense hawks, though, seem sure to support an extended U.S. presence. Connecticut independent Joseph I. Lieberman, a Senate Armed Services member, said a longer but ultimately more successful withdrawal is far preferable to a "rigid withdrawal schedule" that could jeopardize the stability achieved in the past few years.

John McCain of Arizona, ranking Republican on Armed Services, has an even more expansive view of the potential U.S. military role in Iraq. Although that view cost him dearly during his 2008 presidential campaign—when he advocated staying for 100 years or more—McCain still likens the benefits of staying in Iraq to those of keeping thousands of troops in Germany and Japan since World War II and in South Korea since the Korean War ended. "It's not the U.S. presence that matters," he said. "The key, overriding concern for Americans is American casualties."

Officials have pointed to the striking drop in combat casualties as a promising sign. "The Iraqi population remains exhausted from fighting and reluctant to return to communal warfare," Kahl said. Al Qaeda in Iraq "is weaker than ever. Joint terror operations are more active than ever," and Iraqi security forces are getting better all the time—although he concedes that the progress on security ought not yet be labeled "enduring."

STABILITY VS. VIOLENCE

Among the obstacles to stability are the limitations of the Iraqi Security Forces, or ISF, the more than 664,000 members of which are facing a large array of potential factional opposition: as many as 100,000 former Sunni insurgents, about 75,000 Kurdish Peshmerga and perhaps 40,000 Shiite members of radical cleric Moqtada al-Sadr's Iran-backed Jaish al-Mahdi militia.

"For these groups, the choice of peaceful politics over fighting has been a matter of strategic calculation rather than of outright defeat or transforming enlightenment," a Rand Corp. study concluded last month. "To the extent that U.S. military power helped contain or deter these factions, U.S. withdrawal could increase their opportunities to achieve their goals through force, especially if the ISF is not yet up to the task of defeating them."

Levin said he plans to monitor whether Iraq is working toward political reconciliation among its various factions, especially between Arabs and Kurds in the disputed territories in the north. To date, Sunni, Shiite and Kurdish factions appear content to find answers to their grievances through the political process.

Indeed, the Sunnis, who boycotted the 2005 parliamentary elections, are poised to achieve even greater representation in the next government. But while increased Sunni engagement is desirable, such a development could trigger a Kurdish backlash. "Sunni-Shi'a rapprochement could aggravate Kurdish marginalization from an increasingly Arab-dominated political order and the ISF, making Kurd-Arab conflict more probable," the Rand study found. "Iraq could thus break along ethnic instead of sectarian lines, with an Arab core determined to exercise control of the Iraqi state—and Arab interests— and the Kurds equally determined to resist."

Pentagon officials concede that there have been several near misses around Khanaqin and Kirkuk, where Peshmerga and ISF forces nearly clashed. To avert such potential conflicts, the United States is working closely with the United Nations to find a workable solution to Arab-Kurdish disputes involving territory and oil revenue, something Levin says he supports. Meanwhile, the U.S. military intends to locate a majority of its advise-and-assist brigades in northern Iraq, along the Arab-Kurdish fault line.

U.S. commanders have also created so-called combined security mechanisms, which are a series of joint U.S.-ISF-Peshmerga checkpoints, patrols and training efforts around three major areas along that fault line: the cities of Mosul and Kirkuk, and Diyala province. "It's not a permanent solution, and it's not envisioned as such," Kahl said. But such mechanisms are seen as a confidence-building measure to help the United States disengage. In the interim, they are designed to prevent miscalculation that could lead to conflict.

There are those in Congress who appear willing to wait as long as it takes. McCain said the United States still has a long way to go before reaching the finish line. "In the months ahead, as U.S. troops return home, we must deepen and expand America's diplomatic and economic engagement with Iraq," he said on the Senate floor on March 8. "In the years ahead, the United States, especially our Congress, has a responsibility to continue providing the critical support, including the necessary resources to strengthen Iraq's young democracy."

Another threat to the fledgling democracy could come from disgruntled members of executed dictator Saddam Hussein's Baath Party, which is now based in Syria. Some Baathists have worked in the past with Al Qaeda in Iraq, which is weakened but is still a potential threat. Hamza Shareef, the director general of international policy in the Iraqi National Security Council, called the "perverted relationship" between the two groups one of convenience. He suggested, however, that Baathists would never permit Al Qaeda in Iraq to become more powerful than their group.

These extremists are seen as the most likely to stage suicide bombings, but the Iraqi political system has displayed a growing resilience to such attacks. "An order exists—shaky, but increasingly resistant to being blown up, figuratively and literally, by rejectionists and extremists outside it," the Rand study said.

More worrying, said Levin, is the concern that members of some of Iraq's most powerful parties were using the Baathist label as a way to smear political opponents. Controversy erupted during the election when some candidates were excluded because of alleged Baathist ties; some experts fear that such disputes could reignite sectarian tensions.

But other groups that have caused instability in the past, including Shiite militias, appear greatly diminished. "They no longer target civilians on a wide scale," Kahl said. "Al-Sadr has disbanded the Mahdi Army, concentrating residual military activity in a smaller group, which is backed by Iran."

TEHRAN LOOMING

Perhaps the biggest wild card is Iraq's neighbor, Iran. As one of the biggest beneficiaries of the end of the Saddam regime, Tehran has been flexing its muscles throughout the region, including persistently meddling in the Iraqi political scene. Many lawmakers, government officials and experts are quietly pushing for U.S. troops to stay in Iraq to help counter the Iranian influence—both inside Iraq and even in the wider Middle East.

"People don't like to talk about it," said Thomas Donnelly, the director of the Center for Defense Studies at the American Enterprise Institute. "There are a number of gorillas in the room, but this one is a big one."

Whatever decision is taken on the long-term military presence in Iraq, Iran will be watching. A U.S. military force "is an expression of American interest, American influence, American power, America's commitment to the region," Donnelly said. "It also has genuine military value in the reconstruction of the Iraqi military and the Iraqi state. It is not purely symbolic."

But other analysts, and some lawmakers, argue that the best way to counterbalance Iran would be to help build a strong, stable and democratic Iraq. "When Iranians look at a democratic Iraq today amid violent and bloody military crackdowns in their own country, they must be thinking: 'Why not us?'" McCain said.

Iran, for its part, has worked consistently to undermine U.S. efforts in Iraq as well as the Iraqi government. "Iran continues to fund, train, equip, and give some direction to residual Shia militias and extremist elements in Iraq," warned the Pentagon's most recent quarterly report to Congress on Iraq.

U.S. and Iraqi officials acknowledge that Iran has influence over Iraq—Shareef said Iran has thousands of operatives in Iraq—but not control. Many Iraqis, with painful memories of the bloody eight-year war with Iran in the 1980s, remain deeply suspicious of Tehran. And there have been several instances in which the Iraqi government has rejected Iran's overtures: Maliki pushed back against the Iran-backed Mahdi militia in 2008, Iranian-backed parties performed weakly in last year's provincial elections, and Iran was unable to get all the Shiite parties to run on a single list in this month's parliamentary elections.

In fact, some experts say Iran doesn't factor all that heavily into Iraqi security thinking. "If civil war ensued between Shia and Sunni, and the Sunnis started massacring large numbers of Shiites, then Iran might be involved," said Kenneth Katzman, a Congressional Research Service specialist on the Middle East. "I don't see any Iraqi leaders talking about something that would have day-to-day impact."

Growing tension between Washington and Tehran over Iran's nuclear ambitions could end up driving events. The House in December and the Senate in January passed legislation that would impose a broad range of economic sanctions against Iran. The Senate's is more expansive, with language that would direct the president to freeze assets of Iranian officials and prohibit the U.S. government from providing contracts to companies that supply Iran with communications monitoring technology. The House bill focuses on companies that do business in Iran's petroleum sector.

While many lawmakers appear to agree about sanctions, there are disagreements over what impact U.S. forces in Iraq might have on the dispute between Iran and the United States. Levin and Reed argue that any continued presence of U.S. forces in Iraq could be exploited as a propaganda tool for Iran in the Middle East and as a recruitment tool for terrorists. Scowcroft pointed out that U.S. forces there could also be quite vulnerable. If the United States took some kind of military action against Iran, he added, it would probably seek to retaliate in Iraq.

"I don't see U.S. troops in Iraq as the unsinkable aircraft carrier," he said.

Extending Our Stay in Iraq[*]

By Thomas E. Ricks
The New York Times, February 24, 2010

Iraq's March 7 national election, and the formation of a new government that will follow, carry huge implications for both Iraqis and American policy. It appears now that the results are unlikely to resolve key political struggles that could return the country to sectarianism and violence.

If so, President Obama may find himself later this year considering whether once again to break his campaign promises about ending the war, and to offer to keep tens of thousands of troops in Iraq for several more years. Surprisingly, that probably is the best course for him, and for Iraqi leaders, to pursue.

Whether or not the elections bring the long-awaited political breakthrough that genuinely ends the fighting there, 2010 is likely to be a turning-point year in the war, akin to the summer of 2003 (when the United States realized that it faced an insurgency) and 2006 (when that insurgency morphed into a small but vicious civil war and American policy came to a dead end). For good or ill, this is likely the year we will begin to see the broad outlines of post-occupation Iraq. The early signs are not good, with the latest being the decision over the weekend of the leading Sunni party, the National Dialogue Front, to withdraw from the elections.

The political situation is far less certain, and I think less stable, than most Americans believe. A retired Marine colonel I know, Gary Anderson, just returned from Iraq and predicts a civil war or military coup by September. Another friend, the journalist Nir Rosen, avers that Iraq is on a long-term peaceful course. Both men know Iraq well, having spent years working there. I have not seen such a wide discrepancy in expert views since late 2005.

The period surrounding the surge of 2007 has been misremembered. It was not about simply sending 30,000 more troops to Iraq; it was about using force differently, moving the troops off big bases to work with Iraqi units and live among the people. Perhaps even more significantly, the surge signaled a change in American attitudes, with more humility about what could be done, more willingness to listen to Iraqis, and with quietly but sharply reduced ambitions.

The Bush administration's grandiose original vision of transforming Iraq into a beacon of democracy that would alter the Middle East and drain the swamps of terrorism was scuttled and replaced by the more realistic goal of getting American forces out and leaving behind a country that was somewhat stable and, with luck, perhaps democratic and respectful of human rights. As part of the shift, the American commander, Gen. David Petraeus, also effectively put the Sunni insurgency on the American payroll.

Looking back now, I think the surge was the right thing to do. In rejecting the view of the majority of his military advisers and embracing the course proposed by a handful of dissidents, President Bush found his finest moment. That said, the larger goal of the surge was to facilitate a political breakthrough, which has not happened.

All the existential questions that plagued Iraq before the surge remain unanswered. How will oil revenue be shared among the country's major groups? What is to be the fundamental relationship between Shiites, Sunnis and Kurds? Will Iraq have a strong central government or be a loose confederation? And what will be the role of Iran (for my money, the biggest winner in the Iraq war thus far)?

Unfortunately, all of these questions have led to violence in the past, and could again just as the Obama administration's timeline calls for troops to leave areas that are far from quiet. The plan this year is to pull out about 10,000 troops a month for five months, beginning in late spring. That will halve the American military presence, with the remainder (other than a "residual force" of unspecified size) scheduled to be withdrawn in 2011. The withdrawal plan was written on the assumption that the elections would be held late in 2009 or early in 2010. Under the plan, troop numbers would be kept level to ensure stability in a vulnerable period, especially if the Sunnis were to feel that the electoral process was unfair, or if they were not given a role in the new government commensurate with their success at the polls.

But given the changed timetable, just as Iraqi political leaders are struggling to form a new government, American military leaders will be distracted by the myriad tasks of supervising major troop movements. On top of that, the deeper the troop withdrawals go, the more potentially destabilizing they will be—because the first withdrawals will be made in areas that are considered more secure, or where Iraqi forces are deemed more reliable or evenhanded.

By June, American troops may be leaving areas that are far from quiet, and where new tensions may be brewing as a result of the elections. Once again, the United States would be rushing toward failure in Iraq, as it did so often under the Bush administration, trying to pass responsibility to Iraqi officials and institutions before they are ready for the task.

By late summer, the Obama administration could find itself in the uncomfortable position of reconsidering its vows to get out of combat in Iraq by August and to remove all troops by the end of next year. This will be politically difficult for the president, but he has shown admirable flexibility in his handling of Iraq. My impression is that the American people now wish they had never heard of Iraq, but understand just what a mess it is and are willing to give the president a surprising amount of leeway.

Extending the American military presence will be even more politically controversial in Iraq, and for that reason, it would be best to let Iraqi leaders make the first public move to re-open the status of forces agreement of 2008, which calls for American troops to be out of the country by the end of next year. But I think leaders in both countries may come to recognize that the best way to deter a return to civil war is to find a way to keep 30,000 to 50,000 United States service members in Iraq for many years to come.

These troops' missions would be far narrower than during the surge era; their primary goal would be to train and advise Iraqi security forces and to carry out counterterrorism missions. (It is actually hard to get below 30,000 and still have an effective force; many troops are needed for logistics, maintenance, medical, intelligence, communications and headquarters jobs, and additional infantry units are then needed to protect the people performing those tasks.)

Such a relatively small, tailored force would not be big enough to wage a war, but it might be enough to deter a new one from breaking out. An Iraqi civil war would likely be a three- or four-sided affair, with the Shiites breaking into pro- and anti-Iranian factions. It could also easily metastasize into a regional war. Neighboring powers like Turkey and Iran are already involved in Iraqi affairs, and the Sunni Arab states would be unlikely to stand by and watch a Shiite-dominated regime in Baghdad slaughter the Sunni minority. A regional war in the middle of the world's oil patch could shake the global economy to its foundations and make the current recession look mild.

In addition, a continued American military presence could help Iraq move forward politically. No one there particularly likes having the Americans around, but many groups seem to trust the Americans as honest brokers. And there would be a moral, humanitarian and political benefit: Having American soldiers accompany Iraqi units may improve the behavior of Iraqi forces, discouraging relapses to Saddam Hussein-era abuses, or the use of force for private ends and feuds. Advisers not only instruct Iraqi commanders, they also monitor them.

As a longtime critic of the American invasion of Iraq, I am not happy about advocating a continued military presence there. Yet, to echo the counterinsurgency expert David Kilcullen, just because you invade a country stupidly doesn't mean you should leave it stupidly. The best argument against keeping troops in Iraq is the one some American military officers make, which is that a civil war is inevitable, and that by staying all we are doing is postponing it. That may be so, but I don't think it is worth gambling to find out.

The Rationale for Keeping U.S. Forces in Iraq[*]

By Jeremy R. Hammond
Foreign Policy Journal, February 25, 2010

With the deadline for the withdrawal of U.S. troops from Iraq at the end of next year creeping nearer, the U.S. has to find some way to convince the Iraqi government to allow a continued military presence, which is the likely outcome despite the U.S.-Iraq status of forces agreement containing the deadline.

One means by which this will be accomplished, relabeling "combat forces" something else, perhaps remaining as "military advisers" or something to that effect, has already been discussed. Thomas E. Ricks outlines another rationale for maintaining a military occupation of Iraq in the *New York Times*, offering up a variation on a theme that has been familiar throughout the war that is likely to become a mainstay in the political discourse.

With a national election approaching for Iraq on March 7, Ricks opines that "the results are unlikely to resolve key political struggles that could return the country to sectarianism and violence." Therefore, what "probably is the best course" for President Obama is to "once again break his campaign promises about ending the war, and to offer to keep tens of thousands of troops in Iraq for several more years."

Ricks emphasizes the theme of chaos in his op-ed, even writing that the consequence of U.S. troops withdrawing might be "a civil war."

The notion of the U.S. military presence as a stabilizing influence in Iraq is certainly not unfamiliar, despite all evidence to the contrary, including Iraqi opposition—oftentimes violent—to continued occupation. It's a theme that has also been used to justify the troop surge falsely credited with the decline in violence since 2007.

Ricks suggests that the American public could be persuaded to accept a continued military occupation in Iraq because they "understand just what a mess it is," but adds that "Extending the American military presence will be even more politically controversial in Iraq" than in the U.S. The reason is too obvious to mention, but Ricks does manage to fit it in further down the page. "No one there particularly likes having the Americans around," he concedes in passing, towards the end of his argument for why the Americans should stick around.

As evidence of what "a mess" Iraq is and just how real the threat of "civil war" might be if U.S. forces don't remain to stabilize the country, Ricks writes that "the latest" sign is "the decision over the weekend of the leading Sunni party, the National Dialogue Front, to withdraw from the elections."

Ricks doesn't bother enlightening his readers as to why the party decided to boycott the elections. But the *New York Times* did explain elsewhere that its "two most prominent leaders were disqualified from next month's parliamentary elections in Iraq because of supposed ties to Saddam Hussein's Baath Party" (emphasis added), and that the boycott "was prompted by the disqualification of hundreds of candidates, most of them Sunni, by a parliamentary commission last month."

The party issued a statement declaring that "The National Dialogue Front cannot continue in a political process run by a foreign agenda," a reference to the origins of the commission that disqualified Sunni candidates, although the Times doesn't bother to explain the remark to its readers.

The *Times* did, however, does offer an explanation in a separate article, which noted that the decision to disqualify "515 candidates" was mostly on the basis "of accusations that they retained links to Saddam Hussein's Baath Party" (emphasis added).

The body in question, the *Times* noted, is "the Accountability and Justice Commission, charged with purging the country's government of loyalists of the Baath Party."

Although an appeals court reversed the disqualification of 26 of the candidates, the commission's decisions on the rest were upheld, either through rejection of appeals or failure to appeal in the first place.

Yet another *Times* article offered a few more dots, though again no effort was made to connect them for [. . .] its readers. It stated that "many lawmakers had questioned the murky process by which a committee with disputed authority . . . was able to bar nearly one in six candidates based on evidence that has never been made public."

Additionally, "Some of those disqualified appeared to have only tenuous ties, if any, to the Baath Party, the only official political entity allowed under Mr. Hussein's government and one that dominated social and economic life."

The article cryptically hinted at the commission's origin by stating that "The process for establishing those ties dates from the early months after the American invasion in 2003 when the party was banned after Mr. Hussein's fall."

For a more complete explanation, one may turn to still another *Times* article entitled "The Long, Long Shadow of Early Missteps in Iraq," which actually manages to connect a few dots for its readers. The commission's origin was "Order No. 1," issued by L. Paul Bremer III on his fifth day as the head of the U.S. Coalition Provisional Authority, established after the collapse of the Saddam Hussein regime. That decree banned the Baath Party, a process dubbed "de-Baathification" that helped to spur the Iraqi insurgency.

"Order No. 1 was a beginning that has yet to have an end," the article stated, "a little like America's presence in a land it clumsily sought to cast in its own image." The Accountability and Justice Commission, it explained, is "the legacy of Mr. Bremer's order".

Moreover, we may learn elsewhere, the chairman of the commission is none other than Ahmed Chalabi, the known fabricator who peddled false claims of Iraqi weapons of mass destruction (WMD) to the U.S., including through *Times* reporter Judith Miller.

The commission is dominated "by officials appointed by Prime Minister Nuri Kamal al-Maliki," Kenneth M. Pollack and Michael E. O'Hanlon inform us in an additional *Times* op-ed offering up a few more dots.

The commission's decision, they write, "will do more than just throw a wrench in the works. It will persuade a great many Iraqis that the prime minister or other Shiites, like Mr. Chalabi, are using their control over the electoral mechanics to kneecap their rivals. It may also convince many Sunnis that they will never be allowed to win if they play by the rules, and that violence is their only option."

Echoing Ricks' rationale for maintaining a military presence in Iraq, they add, "If this ban remains in effect, the likelihood of electoral violence will skyrocket, and American soldiers will inevitably be called on to halt it." The U.S. embassy in Baghdad, they write, "is working feverishly to persuade the Iraqis to change course."

The top U.S. commander in Iraq, General Raymond T. Odierno, publicly accused Chalabi and the executive director of the commission, Ali Faisal al-Lami, of being "clearly influenced by Iran". Al-Lami, Odierno added, "has been involved in very nefarious activities in Iraq for some time. It is disappointing that someone like him is put in charge of the de-Ba'athification commission."

In other words, the U.S. is now criticizing both Iraq and Iran for upholding a law the U.S. itself was responsible for decreeing, through a commission the U.S. itself was responsible for establishing, by means of a mandate the U.S. itself was responsible for implementing.

As a result of the supposedly Iranian-influenced decision of the Iraqi commission to carry out its U.S.-dictated mandate, the country is expected to erupt once more into sectarian violence unless the decision to withdraw U.S. forces is reversed so that the U.S. military can save Iraqis, most of whom don't want U.S. forces in their country, from themselves.

This view is expressed by Ricks, who adds that by withdrawing its forces, "the United States would be rushing toward failure in Iraq" by "trying to pass responsibility to Iraqi officials and institutions before they are ready for the task." But there is hope in that both U.S. and Iraqi leaders "may come to recognize that the best way to deter a return to civil war is to find a way to keep 30,000 to 50,000 United States service members in Iraq for many years to come."

Perhaps an indication of what he means by "many years to come," Ricks closes by asserting that "The best argument against keeping troops in Iraq is the one some American military officers make, which is that a civil war is inevitable, and that by staying all we are doing is postponing it. That may be so, but I don't think it is worth gambling to find out."

The logical corollary is that U.S. forces must remain in Iraq for a period of time perhaps shorter than forever, but longer than the foreseeable future, in order to prevent this "inevitable" consequence of withdrawal, which is itself evidence that the Iraqis couldn't get along without the U.S. there to, as Ricks puts it, "help Iraq move forward politically."

In this case, that apparently means disregarding the U.S. "Order No. 1." But never mind the actual origin of this particular crisis. It's a simple enough matter to just attribute it to the backwardness of the Iraqis themselves, or perhaps to the meddlesomeness of neighboring Iran, which, needless to say, isn't on Washington's good side anyways.

Ricks' or a similar rationale is likely to win the day, and by such means the U.S. will work around the status of forces agreement deadline for withdrawal and convince the American people and the Iraqi leadership that it needs to stay.

The Iraqi public is another matter, but, they, after all, require no convincing, since their views simply don't matter, except for possibly factoring in as a minor political obstacle to be overcome.

And so it goes.

Doomsday in Iraq—Is It Really Just Around the Corner?*

The Country May Indeed Devolve into Chaos—But that Could, and Did, Happen with U.S. Troops Still There

By Tom Engelhardt
Los Angeles Times, March 10, 2010

We've now been at war intermittently with Iraq for almost 20 years, and with Afghanistan for 30. It adds up to nearly half a century of experience, all bad.

Yet an expanding crew of Washington-based opiners is calling for President Obama to extend the misery, urging the administration to alter its plans—negotiated in the last months of the George W. Bush administration—for the departure of all American troops from Iraq by the end of 2011. Pulling out on schedule, they argue, would virtually assure civil violence and ethnic bloodletting in Iraq.

According to these doomsayers, our withdrawal as scheduled would encourage Shiite militias to stage a violence-filled comeback. Iranian interference in Iraqi affairs would increase—bringing more violence. And the group Al Qaeda in Iraq would move to fill any power void with its own destructive agenda.

So far, the administration and the military say they still hope to pull out on schedule. But last month, the *Washington Post* reported that the U.S. military has drawn up contingency plans for delaying the agreed-upon withdrawal of all combat troops from the country in August. And national security writer Tom Ricks reported on *Foreign Policy*'s website that the top U.S. commander in Iraq, Army Gen. Ray Odierno, has officially requested that a combat brigade remain in the troubled northern city of Kirkuk after the deadline.

Meanwhile, a chorus of the usual pundits—"warrior journalists," as Tom Hayden calls them—are singing ever-louder warnings that the greatest of all dangers would be premature withdrawal. Ricks, for instance, recommended in the *New York Times* that the Obama administration should "find a way" to keep a "relatively small, tailored force" of 30,000 to 50,000 troops in Iraq "for many years to come." (Those numbers, oddly enough, bring to mind the 34,000 U.S. troops that, according to Ricks in his 2006 bestseller, "Fiasco," Deputy Secretary of Defense Paul Wolfowitz projected as the future U.S. garrison in Iraq in the weeks before the invasion of 2003.)

The Brookings Institution's Kenneth Pollack, who beat the drum for invading Iraq in 2003, now argues against removing "the cast"—his metaphor for the U.S. military presence—on the "broken arm" of Iraq too soon. Kimberly and Frederick Kagan, who also championed the war from the beginning, recently wrote a *Wall Street Journal* article calling for "a long-term military partnership with Iraq beyond 2011," saying the country will not be able to defend itself by then.

Iraq is admittedly a mess. On our watch, the country has crashed and burned, and no one claims that we've put it back together. Multibillions of dollars in reconstruction funds later, the U.S. remains incapable of delivering the simplest things like reliable electricity or potable water to significant parts of the country.

But even as Iraq is in shambles, our confidence in ourselves, our—why not say it?—narcissism, remains intact. We are still, somehow, staring into that pool, enamored with the kindly, helpful face that stares back. We have convinced ourselves that we can see the future of Iraq, and that an Iraqi future without us would be desolation itself.

What makes the arguments of the warrior pundits particularly potent is the fact that they base them almost entirely on things that have yet to happen and may never happen. After all, humans have such a lousy track record as predictors of the future. History regularly surprises us.

Few remember anymore, but we went through a version of this 40 years ago in Vietnam. In that conflict too, Americans were repeatedly told that the U.S. couldn't withdraw because, if we left, the enemy would launch a "blood bath" in South Vietnam. This future blood bath of the imagination appeared in innumerable official speeches and accounts. It became so real that it sometimes seemed to put the actual, ongoing blood bath in Vietnam in the shade, and for years it provided a winning explanation for why any departure would have to be interminably and indefinitely delayed.

But when the last American took that last helicopter out, the blood bath didn't happen.

In Iraq, only one thing is really known: After our invasion, and with U.S. and allied troops occupying the country in significant numbers, the Iraqis did descend into a monumental blood bath. It happened in our presence, on our watch, and in significant part thanks to us.

But why should the historical record be taken into account when our pundits and strategists have such privileged access to an otherwise unknown future? In the year to come, based on what we're seeing now, such arguments are likely to intensify. Terrible prophesies about Iraq's future without us will multiply.

It's true that terrible things may happen in Iraq. They could happen while we are there. They could happen with us gone. But history delivers its surprises more regularly than we imagine—even in Iraq.

In the meantime, it's worth keeping in mind that not even Americans can occupy the future. It belongs to no one.

Hope and Change in Iraq[*]

The Elections Show a Functioning Democracy,
If They Can Keep It

By Reuel Marc Gerecht
The Weekly Standard, March 22, 2010

In Iraq we are now where we should have been in 2005 if the Sunni Arab community had not staged a bloody revanchist insurrection. The parliamentary elections on March 7 gave us a good snapshot of the real Iraq: an insecure Sunni Arab minority more or less united in one bloc, the Shiite Arab majority building self-confidence and naturally fracturing along religious/secular lines, and the Kurdish (predominantly Sunni) minority united against the Arabs but internally fractious and increasingly dissatisfied with the two families who've ruled Kurdish politics for decades.

At first glance, we've got a four-way horse race, where shifting coalitions could produce surprising results (a Kurdish-religious Shiite coalition, a Sunni Arab-secular Shiite coalition, or even a Sunni Arab-Kurdish alliance, for example). Although the returns aren't final at this writing, it appears Shiite prime minister Nuri al-Maliki's State of Law slate has come in first; the Iraqiya coalition, which represents Arab Sunnis and some secular Shiites, a close second; and the National Alliance, which pulls together a wide array of Shiites, especially from the more religious south, a close third. The Kurds, meanwhile, split their vote between the Kurdish Alliance, which is the disputatious marriage of the Barzani and Talabani political machines, and the feisty independent Change Movement led by Nawshirwan Mustafa.

If this outcome had been reached in 2005 we all could have popped the champagne. Instead, in 2005, only the Shiite Arabs and Kurds went en masse to the urns. Since then we've had three years of hell and one year of purgatory (Muslims have no intermediate stage between heaven and hell, but the new Iraq is going politically and theologically where no Arabs have gone before). Most pivotally, we had the Battle of Baghdad in 2006–07.

If Iraq continues down a democratic path, the results of that battle—not the presence of U.S. troops over the last seven years—will likely prove to have decided the country's fate. We will soon get to see whether Iraq's Sunni Arabs really can live with the military defeat they suffered in 2007 and the political defeat they suffered last week. We will soon get to see if they can live without the Americans (who, in a truly surreal turnaround, are now the protectors of the very Sunni Arabs who once drove the insurgency against the invader). Politically, the Iraqi Shia are unlikely to be generous with their erstwhile Sunni overlords. Washington can continue to encourage them to be so. But in Iraqi Shiite eyes what Washington has been doing since the surge began in 2007—when General David Petraeus started paying Sunni tribes to stand against al Qaeda and with the Americans—is bribing the Sunnis to behave. The administrations of George W. Bush and Barack Obama have wanted, truth be told, the Shia to accept a kind of affirmative action: For peace and a quicker American withdrawal, we've wanted the Shia to give the Arab Sunnis political and economic guarantees that exceed Sunni Arab electoral power. (The Arab Sunni community represents at most 20 percent of Iraq's population, the Shiite Arabs about 60 percent, and the Kurds the remaining 20 percent.)

In a very Arab way, the Americans have been trying to fight sectarianism through a reward system based on sect. Good democrats that we are, Americans don't say this. But ideally that's what we'd like to see: a firm informal understanding that gives the Arab Sunnis a political check on the Shiite majority. Such an arrangement has become ever more appealing in Washington as the specter of Iranian influence in Iraq has risen. Although Washington's foreign-policy establishment is usually too sophisticated to say flatly that Shiite equals pro-Persian, a pro-Arab-Sunni reflex is deeply embedded in the State Department, the Central Intelligence Agency, the Pentagon, and much of the think tank world that feeds the government. It's an odd view, given the history of relations between Iraqi and Iranian Shiites, which have been defined by suspicion, animosity, and envy more than brotherly love. Still, it persists.

Deeply scarred by Baathist rule and savage insurgent Sunni attacks, and well aware of the disastrous economic state of their religious brethren in southern Iraq, the Iraqi Shiite political establishment will likely give the Sunnis no more than what their numbers demand in parliament (and that may not be much). No matter what happens in the formation of a new government, the Shia are unlikely to increase state subventions to Sunni Arab paramilitary organizations—the anti-al Qaeda "Sons of Iraq" groups that the Americans want incorporated into the Iraqi Army and that the Shiite community deeply distrusts. The pre-election disqualification of some Sunni candidates was probably in part a bit of Shiite electoral hanky-panky against popular Sunni leaders, who may or may not have a bothersome Baathist background. But it was above all an assertion of Shiite determination that "never again" means "never again."

It's a strong bet that these disqualifications—which do not seem to have depressed Sunni participation—are highly popular among the Shia. Ahmad Chalabi, a leader of the National Alliance, whom the American press and Washington's top general in Iraq, Raymond Odierno, described as an Iranian-guided Beelzebub behind the effort to blacklist Sunni Arab candidates, undoubtedly gained in popularity among the Shia from the American onslaught against him. (It is astonishing to see American officials, who have before labeled Chalabi an Iranian agent only to see him rise like Lazarus, repeat the same mistake. Former secretary of state Condoleezza Rice and her aide Robert Blackwill had the excuse of near total ignorance of Iraq and Chalabi; General Odierno and Ambassador Christopher Hill should know better.)

But the Arab Sunnis will have peace—if they want it. There is absolutely no detectable desire among Iraq's Arab Shia for a renewed war against their Sunni compatriots. Even the Sadrists, who led the fiercest, vengeful death-squads against the Sunni community, give no hint that they want combat again with the Sunnis. (The same cannot be said when the Sadrists talk about Prime Minister Maliki, who led the army against them in Baghdad and in Basra.) The Sadrists have dropped the Shiite millenarian language that once scared the Sunnis. Moktada al-Sadr, exiled in Iran, is, as he probably knows, testing the historic Shiite idea of *gheibat*, "absence," where a spiritual leader disappears and then returns to lead the faithful. Democracy isn't kind to absentee politicians, which is, no doubt, why Sadr himself spread rumors of his return to Iraq. But neither he nor his movement is a threat to Iraqi democracy. The Sadrists still have some street power and passion and the possibility of a political impact if the plight of the Shiite poor worsens. But they are playing the democratic game. Only a renewed Sunni attack against the Shia will re-radicalize them.

The Shia won the Battle of Baghdad, and they are increasingly confident they could win any future war—much more decisively, thanks to American training of the Shiite-led Iraqi Army. Rather than give the Sunnis an equal share in government, which is what Sunni politicians really want, the Shia would probably fight. But there is likely considerable political wiggle room between Sunni revanchist dreams and Shiite stubbornness. The Sunni Arab community now has a political voice in the Iraqiya slate, headed by the longtime favorite son of the Central Intelligence Agency, the über-secularist and nominally Shiite Ayad Allawi. This is a much more potent, appealing, and flexible coalition than its predecessor, al-Tawafuq, which proved too lame, too religious, and too authoritarian. It's not clear now how Iraqiya could compromise sufficiently with the Kurds (Iraqiya's Sunni Arab core is vehemently opposed to Kurdish autonomy) or even with Maliki's party to gain real political power (Maliki, no less than Chalabi, is strongly opposed to

de-de-Baathification and obviously doesn't care for putting more Sunni militiamen on the state payroll as soldiers).

But Shiites and Sunnis could work incremental deals. Public largesse could
probably be increased for Sunnis. Not much, though, since Iraq still has very
little cash in relation to the country's needs and the price of oil. Giving the
Sunnis too much—considering that they are vastly better off than southern
Shiites, parts of whose region look as if they just exited the Stone Age—
would likely be political death for a Shiite politician. But small deals might
be enough to keep Sunni elders content, if not thrilled. As Iraq's oil and gas
revenues rise, as they will one of these days, that stress is likely to ease, and
incremental gains could become substantial. And as odd as it might sound,
Chalabi the patrician is more likely to help the process of Sunni-Shiite reconciliation than most other senior Shiite politicians, many of whose families
were truly savaged by the Baath. Chalabi is an old-school Iraqi. He can wax
(ahistorically) poetic about Iraq in the 1950s, before the Hashemite monarchy fell. That's a good thing. He has memories of Sunnis and Shiites in
happier times, the movers and shakers of Iraq gathered around his father's
dining room table and swimming pool. Like all patricians, he sees the world
through families and a socially and intellectually complex matrix that does
not discriminate rigorously by creed. Chalabi is never one to waste a political opportunity, but he is also a man of profound sentiment. His sentiments
encompass Sunnis. With Shiite politicians, that is not always the case.

The issue really is Sunni expectations. The March 7 elections raised them.
Allawi did his side no favors by often suggesting that things could change dramatically under his leadership. The next few months will be telling as politicians come down to earth after the campaign. If the Sunnis can live with the
fact that a democratic Iraq will always disappoint their clannish aspirations
for political preeminence and a right to live off state subsidies, then Iraq's future is pretty bright. The Americans really ought to have one overwhelming
goal: hang around. Not in large numbers. The drawdown of U.S. troops is
a good idea. But we should view Iraq the same way we viewed postwar Germany, France, and Italy. The presence of American troops was the ultimate
guarantor that those countries would not slip back into dictatorship.

Washington shouldn't choose sides in Iraq, and it shouldn't intervene in
Iraqi politics except *in extremis*. But we do want to be there, in the background, as we were in Europe. Even Shiite politicians who vociferously oppose an American troop presence can privately suggest a more nuanced view.
As the journalist Tom Ricks has suggested, American combat troops could
be given a more anodyne label—stabilization forces, a support presence. Our
training mission with the Iraqi Army and police is going to take years. Needless to say, most Sunnis will be thrilled. The problem will be with the Shia.
We've not played Shiite politics brilliantly (as the stupid war against Chalabi
demonstrates). But a constructive, unobtrusive U.S. presence is doable if the
Obama administration handles the issue deftly.

If the White House really is worried that Iraq could become an Iranian satrapy, that's another reason for a small but potent U.S. military force to stay there. Iraqi democracy is a big deal. The American left and right, which have dismissed its evolution and belittled the American achievement in giving it birth, are stuck in the past, in an unchanging Middle East that never existed. What's happened in Iraq since 2003—and what's happened in Iran since last June 12—really ought to plant the possibility that the Islamic Middle East isn't a hopeless case. Some change there just might be progress. Accepting this will cause indigestion for those who've been unalterably attached to the image of post-Saddam Iraq as "the biggest strategic failure in American history" and who've denounced the pointlessness of promoting democracy "through the barrel of a gun." Unfortunately, Barack Obama once belonged to this group. But as president he has proven flexible in foreign affairs. With him, as with Iraq after another successful election—freer and more competitive than any election in the history of the Middle East—there are reasons to hope.

Long Goodbye, But Goodbye*

Elections Shaky, But Iraq Withdrawal Necessary

The Palm Beach Post, March 16, 2010

What is an AAB? If Iraq's March 7 election is a success, by the end of August Americans will be familiar with the now-obscure acronym.

AAB stands for "Advise and Assist Brigade." By Sept. 1, it's supposed to be the predominant type of U.S. military unit remaining in Iraq. Combat troops, President Obama has promised, will be gone by then.

By some measures, Iraq's parliamentary election already has been a success. The turnout was about 62 percent. Many Sunnis who boycotted previous elections voted in this one. Fewer than 40 people were killed in election day violence. Results are slow coming in, but signs are that Prime Minister Nouri al-Maliki or former Prime Minister Ayad Allawi will lead the new government. Both are secular Shiites; religious parties have not fared as well.

The Obama administration already has begun withdrawing troops. President Bush's "surge," announced more than three years ago, increased American forces to 171,000 from 132,000. Mr. Bush never could reduce forces to below the pre-surge level, but Mr. Obama has cut the number to 96,000. By the end of August, only 50,000 are supposed to remain in those AABs. Then, for the real challenge, the United States and Iraq have agreed that all American forces should be out by the end of 2011.

This week marks the seventh anniversary of the invasion. So even if U.S. troops leave on schedule, the war will have lasted almost nine years. May 1, by the way, will be the seventh anniversary of Mr. Bush's "Mission Accomplished" stunt flight to the USS *Abraham Lincoln*. We note these anniversaries to make clear how little standing former Vice President Dick Cheney's camp has to criticize the Obama administration, even if the Iraq deadlines slip or the withdrawal agreement is renegotiated to leave 35,000 troops in Iraq more or less permanently. Some analysts call such a development inevitable.

The first time that a soldier fires a weapon in Iraq after August, Bush propagandists may claim that the AAB units are combat forces in disguise. Therefore, President Obama lied. In fact, the real deceit was the Bush-Cheney campaign for the invasion. The administration overstated the weapons case and fabricated a link between Iraq and 9/11.

Because of the Iraq blunder, progress in Afghanistan stalled. Just as the last combat troops leave Iraq, the last of the 30,000 extra U.S. troops Mr. Obama ordered to Afghanistan will arrive there. The war in Afghanistan—where the terrorism threat really lies—by then will have stretched to nine years after the U.S. invasion to drive out the Taliban. A distracting, tragic, expensive war Mr. Bush shouldn't have started might be ending. The war he should have finished long ago continues.

Rebirth of a Nation*

By Babak Dehghanpisheh, John Barry, and Christopher Dickey
Newsweek, March 8, 2010

"Iraqi democracy will succeed," President George W. Bush declared in November 2003, "and that success will send forth the news from Damascus to Tehran that freedom can be the future of every nation." The audience at the National Endowment for Democracy in Washington answered with hearty applause. Bush went on: "The establishment of a free Iraq at the heart of the Middle East will be a watershed event in the global democratic revolution."

In Iraq, meanwhile, an insurgency was growing, terrorism was spreading, and American forces were in a state of near panic. They had begun rounding up thousands of the Iraqis they had come to "liberate," dragging them from their homes in the middle of the night and throwing them into Abu Ghraib Prison. At the time of Bush's speech, some of those detainees were being tortured and humiliated. Iraq had entered a spiral of gruesome violence that would kill scores of thousands of its people and cost more than 4,000 U.S. military personnel their lives. American taxpayers month after month, year after year—and to this day—would spend more than $1.5 billion per week just to keep hundreds of thousands of beleaguered troops on the ground, fearful that if they withdrew too quickly, or at all, the carnage would grow worse and war, not democracy, would spread throughout the region.

Bush's rhetoric about democracy came to sound as bitterly ironic as his pumped-up appearance on an aircraft carrier a few months earlier, in front of an enormous banner that declared MISSION ACCOMPLISHED. And yet it has to be said and it should be understood—now, almost seven hellish years later—that something that looks mighty like democracy is emerging in Iraq. And while it may not be a beacon of inspiration to the region, it most certainly is a watershed event that could come to represent a whole new era in the history of the massively undemocratic Middle East.

The elections to be held in Iraq on March 7 feature 6,100 parliamentary candidates from all of the country's major sects and many different parties. They have wildly conflicting interests and ambitions. Yet in the past couple of years, these politicians have come to see themselves as part of the same club, where hardball political debate has supplanted civil war and legislation is hammered out, however slowly and painfully, through compromises—not dictatorial decrees or, for that matter, the executive fiats of U.S. occupiers. Although protected, encouraged, and sometimes tutored by Washington, Iraq's political class is now shaping its own system—what Gen. David Petraeus calls "Iraqracy." With luck, the politics will bolster the institutions through which true democracy thrives.

Of course, as U.S. Ambassador to Baghdad Christopher Hill says, "the real test of a democracy is not so much the behavior of the winners; it will be the behavior of the losers." Even if the vote comes off relatively peacefully, the maneuvering to form a government could go on for weeks or months. Elections in December 2005 did not produce a prime minister and cabinet until May 2006. And this time around the wrangling will be set against the background of withdrawing American troops. Their numbers have already dropped from a high of 170,000 to fewer than 100,000, and by August there should be no more than 50,000 U.S. soldiers left in the country. If political infighting turns to street fighting, the Americans may not be there to intervene.

Anxiety is high, not least in Washington, where Vice President Joe Biden now chairs a monthly cabinet-level meeting to monitor developments in Iraq. But a senior White House official says the group is now "cautiously optimistic" about developments there. "The big picture in Iraq is the emergence of politics," he notes. Indeed, what's most striking—and least commented upon—is that while Iraqi politicians have proved noisy, theatrical, inclined to storm off and push confrontations to the brink, in recent years they have always pulled back.

Think about what's happened just in the last month. After a Shiite-dominated government committee banned several candidates accused of ties to the Baathist regime of Saddam Hussein, there were fears that sectarian strife could pick up again. Saleh al-Mutlaq, who heads one of the largest Sunni parties, was disqualified. He says he tried complaining to the head of the committee, Ahmad Chalabi, and even met with the Iranian ambassador, thinking Tehran had had a hand in what he called these "dirty tricks"—but to no avail.

Two weeks later Mutlaq nervously paced the garden of the massive Saddam-era Al-Rashid Hotel as he weighed his dwindling options. "I got a call from the American Embassy today," he said, grimly. "They said, 'Most of the doors are closed. There's nothing left for us to work.'" He shook his head. "The American position is very weak."

But what's most interesting is what did not happen. There was no call for violence, and Mutlaq soon retracted his call for a boycott. The elections remain on track. Only about 150 candidates were ultimately crossed off the electoral lists. No red-faced Sunni politicians appeared on television ranting about a Shiite witch hunt or Kurdish conspiracy. In fact, other prominent Sunni politicians have been conspicuous for their low profile. Ali Hatem al-Suleiman, a tough, flamboyant Sunni sheik who heads the powerful Dulaim tribe in Anbar province, is running for Parliament on a list with Shiite Prime Minister Nuri al-Maliki. He scoffs at effete urban pols like Mutlaq: "They represent nothing. Did they join us in the fight against terrorists? We are tribes and have nothing to do with them."

What outsiders tend to miss as they focus on the old rivalries among Shiites, Sunnis, and Kurds is that sectarianism is giving way to other priorities. "The word 'compromise' in Arabic—mosawama—is a dirty word," says Mowaffaq al-Rubaie, who served for many years as Iraq's national-security adviser and is running for Parliament. "You don't compromise on your concept, your ideology, your religion—or if you do," he flicked his hand dismissively, "then you're a traitor." Rubaie leans in close to make his point. "But we learned this trick of compromise. So the Kurds are with the Shia on one piece of legislation. The Shia are with the Sunnis on another piece of legislation, and the Sunnis are with the Kurds on still another."

The turnaround has been dramatic. "The political process is very combative," says a senior U.S. adviser to the Iraqi government who is not authorized to speak on the record. "They fight—but they get sufficient support to pass legislation." Some very important bills have stalled, most notably the one that's meant to decide how the country's oil riches are divvied up. But as shouting replaces shooting, the Parliament managed to pass 50 bills in the last year alone, while vetoing only three. The new legislation included the 2010 budget and an amendment to the investment law, as well as a broad law, one of the most progressive in the region, defining the activities of nongovernmental organizations.

The Iraqis have surprised even themselves with their passion for democratic processes. In 2005, after decades living in Saddam Hussein's totalitarian "republic of fear," they flooded to the polls as soon as they got the chance. Today Baghdad is papered over with campaign posters and the printing shops on Saadoun Street seem to be open 24 hours a day, cranking out more. Political cliques can no longer rely on voters to rubber-stamp lists of sectarian candidates. Those that seem to think they still might, like the Iranian-influenced Islamic Supreme Council of Iraq, have seen their support wane dramatically. Provincial elections a year ago were dominated by issues like the need for electricity, jobs, clean water, clinics, and especially security. Maliki has developed a reputation for delivering some of that, and his candidates won majorities in nine of 18 provinces. They lead current polls as well.

The word skeptics like to fall back on is "fragile." No one can say for sure whether the Iraqis' political experiment is sustainable. Many U.S. officials see themselves as the key players who hold everything together, massaging egos and nudging adversaries closer together. Some are already talking about revising the schedule whereby all U.S. troops would leave the country in 2011.

But the greater risk may be having the Americans see themselves as indispensable. The fiercely nationalistic Iraqi public still chafes at U.S. interference and resents any Iraqi politicians who seem to be too much in Washington's pockets. Ali Allawi, who was minister of finance and minister of defense early in the post-Saddam government, describes the current scene in Iraq as a "minimalist" democracy built around a "new class" of 500 to 600 politicians. The Middle East has seen this kind thing before, he says, in Egypt and Iraq under British tutelage in the first half of the last century. Then, the elites learned to play party politics, too, but not to meet the needs of the people. "That ended in tears," says Allawi.

In Iraq today, conditions seem more likely to reinforce than to undermine the gains so far. Iraqis have been hardened by a very tough past and now, coming out the other side of the infernal tunnel that is their recent history, many share a sense of solidarity as survivors. "Identities in Iraq are fluid, but there is more of a sense of an Iraqi national identity," says Middle East historian Phebe Marr, whose first research trip to the country was in 1956.

You notice this, for instance, at the Iraqi National Symphony Orchestra, where conductor Karim Wasfi manages to extract harmony from Kurds, Christians, Sunnis, Shiites, and Bahais. Some of the women musicians wear the hijab, or headscarf; others do not. During the height of sectarian violence in 2006, almost half of the orchestra fled the country. Those who stayed behind got death threats, and one was killed. During one concert they had to play against the contrapuntal percussion of a firefight just outside the hall— but play they did. "It was about survival," says Wasfi.

Wasfi now says there are audiences asking for the symphony to perform even in conservative religious towns like Karbala, in southern Iraq. And bigger cities like Baghdad and Basra are regaining their old cosmopolitan airs. Abu Nawas Street along the Tigris River is once again lit up with lively restaurants serving broiled fish and beer. Liquor stores that had closed up shop during the height of the civil war now stack cases of Heineken and boxes of Johnny Walker Black in front of their doors. University students, once cowed by militias like the Mahdi Army, are feeling freer. Sawsan Abdul Rahman, an English major at Mustansiriyah University, says in the past she felt obliged to cover her head. "I wear a miniskirt now," she says.

The changes are more than superficial. As economist Douglass North pointed out last year in his influential book *Violence and Social Orders*, the key to building stable societies is to create a web of institutions that people can fall back on when governments, or mere politics, fail. Iraq is beginning to do just that. The country not only has the freest press in the region, but the gutsiest. More than 800 newspapers and TV and radio stations have aggressively gone after politicians and sleazy businessmen. The country now has more than 1,200 trained judges, and courts have convicted senior officials on corruption charges, with more cases pending. Women's groups, too, have asserted themselves, pushing for 25 percent of provincial councils to be female and forcing the Education Ministry to roll back a proposal to separate boys and girls in school.

Perhaps the most encouraging sign is that Iraq's military has become one of the most respected institutions in the country. The remnants of Al Qaeda in Iraq continue to carry out horrendous suicide operations, and some analysts expect the terrorists to step up their activities if sectarian tensions increase, and as American troops withdraw. But they no longer seem to pose an existential threat to the central government, and have inspired near-universal revulsion among Iraqis. Nor do most close observers fear the opposite—that the Army might become too strong and mount a coup. "I think people mention this because it's been such a recurrent theme in Iraq's past," says Ambassador Hill. "But we're certainly not seeing signs that the military is interested in engaging in politics."

Retired U.S. Army Lt. Gen. James Dubik, who was in charge of training the Iraqi military in 2007 and 2008, says the more relevant question is whether Iraq's political leaders might try to use the military for sectarian purposes. Prime Minister Maliki, who directly controls some counterterrorism forces, has been accused of targeting Sunni rivals using those troops. But, says Dubik, Iraqi commanders are "very much attuned" to the danger, and generally do not launch such missions without broader approval. "They are really trying to develop a mature process."

Neighboring Iran remains a concern. Tehran continues to compete for influence in Iraq using every means at its disposal, including trade, religious ties, diplomacy, and covert links to militias that target U.S. troops. But since Iran's own contested presidential elections last June, its influence has diminished. Seyyed Sadeq, the police chief in the Iraqi city of Al Amarah, is a Shiite who trained with the Iranian-supported Badr Brigades, and was based in Iran throughout the 1990s. Several of his Iraqi friends from those days remained on the Iranian payroll after 2003. Members of the Quds Force, the branch of the Iranian Revolutionary Guards that runs its foreign operations, "used to come here every month or so," says Sadeq. "But recently it's been every six, seven months. I am hearing that Quds Force commanders are busy with the internal operations in Iran so they don't have much time to pay attention to Iraq."

Most important in the long term is the fact that whoever rules in Iraq should be able to take advantage of the country's enormous and largely untapped wealth of oil and natural gas. The Kurds in the north, the Shiites in the south, and now the Sunnis in the west of the country can all lay claim to enormous fields—and even without a hydrocarbon law on the books, the government is finding ways to work with foreign oil companies to exploit these resources. Industry analysts believe Iraq could raise its output from almost 2.5 million barrels a day to 10 million by the end of the decade. Even at current production rates, Iraq's revenues last year were $39 billion.

This is what truly scares Iraq's neighbors. Yes, even the country's fledgling democracy is more vibrant than anywhere else in the region, except perhaps Lebanon (and Iraqis love to point out that America's own system isn't exactly working in textbook fashion right now). But more important, the foundations of a regional power are emerging, one that is equally threatening to Saudi Arabia and to Iran. (Some analysts believe Tehran's nuclear program is meant to intimidate and deter a resurgent Baghdad, not just Washington and Tel Aviv.) Iraq, for better or worse, democratic or not, will be a power to be reckoned with. Such is America's dark victory there.

4

Turkey: Strategic Crossroads

Editor's Introduction

In terms of both culture and geography, Turkey occupies a unique middle ground between Europe and the Middle East. On the one hand, it's a secular democracy and longtime NATO member with hopes of joining the European Union (EU). On the other, its ruling Justice and Development Party has, according to some, shown signs of embracing "Islamist" policies and undermining Turkey's constitutionally mandated separation of church and state. Usually a staunch U.S. ally, Turkey raised eyebrows in 2003, when it refused to let American forces use the country as a staging ground for the invasion of Iraq.

For these and other reasons, U.S.-Turkish relations have grown more complex than they were during the Cold War, when Turkey gamely hosted American nuclear missiles and helped contain the Soviet threat. Given its growing economy and recently implemented "zero problems with neighbors" policy, Turkey is emerging as a regional power. The country is now in a position to mediate between Israel and its Arab neighbors, for example, and negotiate with Iran on the subject of nuclear weapons. While Turkey has said it aims to curb its neighbor's nuclear ambitions, Prime Minister Recep Tayyip Erdogan recently referred to Iranian President Mahmoud Ahmadinejad as his "good friend," leading some to question his allegiances.

The pieces in this chapter don't focus on American troop presence per se, but they do consider how the United States should engage with Turkey. In "Triumph of the Turks," the first selection, Owen Matthews and Christopher Dickey argue that the U.S. war in Iraq has benefited Turkey, creating a "power vacuum" that the relatively stable, prosperous nation is poised to fill. Addressing the question of whether Turkey remains committed to its Western allies, foreign minister Ahmet Davutoglu assures Matthews that "integration with Europe is the main objective of Turkish foreign policy." "But it doesn't mean that because of these strong ties, we can ignore the Middle East, we can ignore Asia, Central Asia, North Africa, or Africa," Davutoglu adds.

Matthews takes a closer look at Erdogan's controversial party in the next entry, "The Army Is Beaten." Having thwarted an attempted coup and asserted its power over the military, the Justice and Development Party is positioned to pursue what Matthews calls a "vision of a more Islamic Turkey," something it will achieve by democratic means, making it difficult for the United States to intervene. "Does the U.S. want Middle East allies who are less democratic but more friendly, or more democratic but more hostile to America?" Matthews asks, indicating a preference for the latter.

In "Testy Erdogan: Turkey and the West," the subsequent piece in this chapter, a writer for *The Economist* maintains that Turkey is more pro-Western than it appears. Even if the country refused to participate in the 2003 invasion of Iraq, the author observes, it has since opened its Incirlik airbase to U.S. supply planes, helping the war effort in a non-combat capacity.

In the following selection, "The Status of U.S. Nuclear Weapons in Turkey," Alexandra Bell and Benjamin Loehrke discuss what it would take to rid Turkey of what's left of its Cold War arsenal, an estimated 90 "gravity bombs" that no longer serve any major strategic purpose. If President Barack Obama wants to achieve his ambitious nuclear-disarmament goals, the authors contend, the United States needs to strengthen diplomatic ties with Turkey, sign weapons-reduction treaties with Russia, and prevent Iran from joining the nuclear club.

In the final article, "Unwelcomed Missiles," Feryaz Ocakli and Yelena Biberman consider why Turkey rejected a missile defense system (MDS) the U.S. military had sought to build within its borders. The writers maintain that Turkey's rationale was twofold. First, the country was hoping it could force the United States to include Russia in the MDS project—a logical move, since Russia is Turkey's leading trading partner. Second, Ocakli and Biberman posit, Turkey's "zero problems with neighbors" policy demands it not do anything Iran might view as aggressive. Since the main purpose of the MDS, at least in the near term, would be guarding against Iranian nuclear strikes, Turkey's participation in the project would likely anger its second-largest trading partner. Again, Turkey finds itself in the middle, not wanting to get caught up in conflicts between the United States and Russia or the United States and Iran.

Triumph of the Turks[*]

Turkey Is the Surprising Beneficiary of U.S. Misadventures in the Middle East

By Owen Matthews and Christopher Dickey
Newsweek, December 7, 2009

Archibald Wavell himself could scarcely have imagined how horribly accurate his prediction would prove to be. Having watched in dismay as the
victorious European powers carved up the Ottoman Empire after World
War I—"the war to end war"—the British officer commented that they had
instead created "a peace to end peace." And sure enough, the decades since
have spawned a succession of colonial misrule, coups, revolutions, and an
epidemic of jihadist violence. The U.S.-led invasion of Iraq in 2003 could
be viewed as a last-ditch attempt by the world's sole remaining superpower
to impose order on the region. Instead, the net result was to create a power
vacuum, leaving Iraq too weak to counterbalance its neighbors and threatening to destabilize the whole map.

Turkey, the old seat of Ottoman power, did its best to stay out of that
fight, refusing even to let U.S. forces cross Turkish soil for the 2003 invasion.
Still, it's the Turks—not the Iranians, as many observers claim—who are now
emerging as the war's real winners. In economic terms Turkey is running
neck and neck with Iran as Iraq's biggest trading partner, even as most U.S.
businesses sit helplessly on the sidelines. And in terms of regional influence,
Turkey has no rival. The country's stern-faced prime minister, Recep Tayyip
Erdogan, is working to consolidate that strength as he asserts Turkey's independence in a part of the world long dominated by America. Next week he's
in Washington to meet with President Obama, but only a few weeks ago he
stood shoulder to shoulder with his "good friend" Mahmoud Ahmadinejad
<u>in Tehran and</u> defended Iran's nuclear program.

That's only one example of the behavior that's disturbing many of Turkey's longtime NATO partners. Among the biggest worries has been the souring of ties with Israel, once Turkey's close ally, over the military offensive in Gaza earlier this year that human-rights groups say killed more than 1,400 Palestinians. Erdogan walked out of the World Economic Forum in protest over the deaths, and recently scrapped a decade-old deal allowing the Israeli Air Force to train over Turkish territory. At the same time, the Turkish prime minister has repeatedly supported Sudan's president, Omar al-Bashir, claiming he couldn't possibly be guilty of genocide in Darfur because he's a "good Muslim." Right now there are "more points of disagreement than of agreement" between Washington and Ankara, says Philip Gordon, Obama's point man on Turkey at the State Department.

What scares Washington most is the suspicion that Ankara's new attitude may be driven less by the practical pursuit of Turkey's national interest than by thinly concealed Islamist ideology. Erdogan has always denied mixing religion and politics, but his ruling Justice and Development Party (known by its Turkish initials, AKP) has been investigated repeatedly by Turkey's top courts on charges of undermining Turkey's constitutional commitment to a strictly secular state. But official policy notwithstanding, Turkish attitudes toward Europe have displayed a marked cooling over the past five years, and a corresponding rise in hostility toward Western institutions like the International Monetary Fund. "No one in the government has made any attempt to reverse rampant anti-Americanism in Turkey," says Kemal Köprülü of the independent ARI think tank. "The government cannot admit it, but most decision making in foreign and domestic policy simply doesn't take Western values into account."

On the other hand, Turks could be excused for thinking that Western decision makers don't always lose sleep over Turkish interests. During the Cold War, Washington did anything necessary to stabilize the region and keep the Kremlin from gaining ground, often backing nominally pro-Western despots like the Shah of Iran and the Turkish generals who seized power from civilian governments three times in as many decades. The result was a disaster for America; it ended up with unreliable allies who were hated by their own people. In Turkey, the cumulative anti-U.S. resentment peaked in 2003 when the Bush administration pressed Ankara to let U.S. forces invade Iraq through Turkish territory—a plan that was derailed only at the last moment by a parliamentary revolt.

That was the low point of Turkey's relationship with the United States. But it was also the start of Turkey's rise to economic recovery and regional influence, and the beginning of a new kind of relationship with Washington. Indeed, Turkey's new standing in the region has a chance of transforming the country into something far more valuable to Washington than a subservient tool or proxy. The Turks say they're seeking to become what Turkish Foreign Minister Ahmet Davutoglu calls a "partner to solve the region's problems." Whatever ambitions they may have harbored in earlier years, it's only in this decade—especially since 2002, when Erdogan and the AKP came to power—that Turkey has had the economic and political strength, as well as the military presence, to fill such a position.

Turkey's economy has more than doubled in the past decade, converting the nation from a backwater to a regional powerhouse. At the same time, its financial focus has moved closer to home: Turkey now conducts more trade with Russia, Iraq, and Iran than it does with the EU. Energy politics have also favored the Turks, who find themselves astride no fewer than three competing energy supply routes to Europe—from Russia, from the Caspian, and from Iran. Years of reform and stability are paying off as well. Ankara is on the verge of a historic deal with its Kurdish minority to end an insurgency that has left 35,000 dead in the past quarter century. In turn, Turkey is making peace with neighboring countries that once supported the insurgents, such as Syria, Iran, and Armenia. The principle is simple, says a senior Erdogan aide who's not authorized to speak on the record: "We can't be prosperous if we live in a poor neighborhood. We can't be secure if we live in a violent one."

The advantages keep compounding. Thanks to judicious diplomacy and expanding business ties throughout the region, Turkey is close to realizing what Davutoglu calls his "zero-problems-with-neighbors policy." The new stance has boosted Ankara's influence even further; the Turks have become the trouble-ridden region's mediators of choice, called in to help with disputes between the Palestinian factions Hamas and Fatah, between Iraq and Syria—even, before Erdogan's outburst in Davos, between Israel and Syria. Speaking at a recent press conference in Rome, Erdogan expressed little hope that Turkey could do more for Syria and Israel. "[Prime Minister Benjamin] Netanyahu doesn't trust us," he said. "That's his choice." But others in the region still welcome Ankara's assistance: Turkish diplomats are excellently trained in conflict resolution.

That can scarcely be said for Iran. The Tehran regime remains paralyzed by infighting and is far from loved in most of the Arab world. Saudis in particular think back fondly to the Ottomans facing off against the Persians, not to mention their feelings about Sunni Turks versus Shiite Iranians. "Saudi Arabia is welcoming the new Turkish comeback," says Jamal Khashoggi, editor of the influential Jidda daily *Al-Watan*. Not the least important part of the charm is that Erdogan's government has a distinctly Islamic (and by Saudi lights, a distinctly Sunni Islamic) coloration—"even if no Turkish officials would say that publicly, because it is politically incorrect," says Khashoggi.

Still, the Turks believe they're wise not to play an antagonistic role, and officials in Ankara insist that Erdogan's warm words to Ahmadinejad are no more than atmospherics. At base, they say, Turkey shares the West's goals regarding Iran's nuclear ambitions; it's just doing things in its own way. "We have been dealing with [Iranians] for centuries," says the Erdogan aide. "We show them the respect and friendship they crave. Would our being hostile to Iran do anything to solve the problem of their nuclear program?" When the International Atomic Energy Agency offered Iran the option of exporting most of its low-enriched uranium in return for French-made fuel rods in October, Erdogan offered Ahmadinejad a deal (apparently with Washington's blessing): Iran could store its uranium in Turkey rather than send it to a non-Muslim country.

Tehran ultimately said no, but the effort demonstrated that Turkey is prepared to do its part to keep the region peaceful and safe. Ankara insists that its new friendships in the region are no threat to its longstanding ties to the West. "NATO is Turkey's strongest alliance, and integration with Europe is the main objective of Turkish foreign policy," insists Davutoglu. "But it doesn't mean that because of these strong ties, we can ignore the Middle East, we can ignore Asia, Central Asia, North Africa, or Africa." The world has changed radically since the fall of the Ottomans, and Turkey is unlikely ever to regain the imperial power it wielded for 350 years, from Algiers to Budapest and Mecca. But as the world tries to move, at last, beyond the 90-year-old peace that ended peace, no other country is better positioned to pick up the pieces.

The Army Is Beaten[*]

Why the U.S. Should Hail the Islamists

By Owen Matthews
Newsweek, March 4, 2010

The political logic should be simple. The arrest of a shadowy group of generals for allegedly plotting a bloody coup should be a victory for justice. The end of military meddling in politics should be a victory for democracy. And greater democracy should make a country more liberal and more pro-European.

Except that in Turkey, political logic doesn't always follow simple patterns. Yes, last week's arrests of dozens of Army officers on charges of plotting bombings and murders are a win for civilian prosecutors over the once untouchable military. More important, the arrests also mark the quiet demise of the military as a decisive force in Turkish politics for the first time in centuries. That's a vital step in Turkey's road to becoming a mature democracy.

But the paradox is that a more democratic Turkey doesn't necessarily mean one that is more pro-European or more pro-American. And with the last major obstacle to the ruling AK Party's power gone, Turkey's conservative prime minister, Recep Tayyip Erdogan, will be free to implement his vision of a more Islamic Turkey. More democracy, then, doesn't necessarily lead to more liberalism, either.

The first victim of the new order may be Europe. Ever since they came to power in 2002, AK Party leaders have used EU membership as a shield to defend their reform programs against attacks from ultrasecularists in the military and the judiciary. Notionally, the military was in favor of joining Europe, so the AK Party railroaded through most of its most radical changes under the EU's banner. Downscaling the powers of the military-dominated

National Security Council, banning the death penalty, scrapping some re-strictions on free speech, allowing Kurdish language rights—all were in the Copenhagen criteria set by the EU. But now that the AK Party's main rival, the military, has been shown to be a paper tiger, there's not much utility for Erdogan & Co. in pushing the European project any further.

That's terrible timing for Europe. Support within the EU for further ex-pansion is fading fast. A looming crisis over Cyprus threatens to create further animosity on both sides as EU members Greece and Greek Cyprus threaten to block Ankara's accession bid. Add to that various tin-eared EU initiatives, like trying to get the conservative Turks to allow gay marriage, and you have a recipe for trouble. Turks are also angry because of the EU's many unful-filled promises over opening Cyprus's ports to international trade. The AK Party's win over the Army could well prove to be the EU's serious loss.

It also raises a tough question for Washington: does the U.S. want Middle East allies who are less democratic but more friendly, or more democratic but more hostile to America? During the Cold War, when the military was in charge, Turkey fell into the first camp. Now it makes sense for Washing-ton to choose democracy—even if the outcomes aren't, as George W. Bush found in Iraq, always pro-Western. Cutting the Army's dead hand from poli-tics will allow Turkey to define secularism democratically and to deal openly with issues like the demands of the Kurdish minority for autonomy. That choice should be particularly easy now, as evidence presented by Turkish prosecutors suggests that the self-declared guardians of Turkey's secular or-der plotted heinous crimes in order to destabilize the AK Party, possibly including the bombing of the British Consulate in Istanbul in 2003.

If Turkey becomes more anti-Western, that's probably inevitable. A storm of popular anger is brewing over the EU's undeclared rejection of Turkish membership, even as the accession process continues, and over moves in the U.S. Congress to recognize the massacres of Ottoman Armenians in 1915 as a genocide. If the vote goes ahead, expect Turks to retaliate, perhaps by refus-ing to support U.S. sanctions against Iran in the U.N. Security Council.

Turks have made it clear repeatedly at the ballot box that they endorse the AK Party's vision of a less-rigorously secular country. Ordinary Turks aren't huge fans of the U.S., either. But it's also clear that Turkey under the AK Party will remain a Western ally, and NATO will remain Ankara's most important strategic partner. How do we know? The AK Party says so, and it has no real options. There's no rival alliance, not with Iran, the Arab world, or Russia, which could possibly rival the clout Turkey has, with the second-largest Army in NATO. In the short term, Turkey will likely sour on the EU and have a loud row with the U.S. over Armenia. In the long term, the downfall of the Army will make Turkey a stronger democracy and a more stable and mature partner. So the world would be wise to side with the AK Party, not seek a return of the discredited generals.

Testy Erdogan[*]

Claims that Turkey Is Drifting Away from the West
Seem Exaggerated

The Economist, December 5, 2009

When Turkey's prime minister, Recep Tayyip Erdogan, meets Barack Obama in the White House next week, he will insist on his country's Western credentials. He will be greeted with a request for more troops to back the American surge in Afghanistan. Turkey, which has NATO's second-biggest army, has 1,700 soldiers on Afghan soil and Turkish generals have led allied forces there. Yet Mr Erdogan's mildly Islamist Justice and Development (AK) Party dislikes American calls to fight fellow Muslims in Afghanistan. Turkey has opted to train Afghan security forces and build roads and schools instead. Mr Erdogan will spurn demands for combat troops.

His Western critics may seize on this as confirmation of Turkey's supposed drift away from the West under seven years of AK rule. Mr Erdogan's cosiness with Iran and Sudan, plus his salvoes against Israel, feed claims that he is an Islamist firebrand at heart. His behaviour has spawned a flurry of hand-wringing in the West.

Yet to Turkish jihadists, who are surfacing in Afghanistan and Chechnya, Mr Erdogan is an American poodle. It was these home-grown militants, with links to al-Qaeda, who in November 2003 killed over 60 people in suicide bombings against British and Jewish targets in Istanbul. If Turkish troops started shooting at fellow Muslims, that would swell the ranks of Islamist radicals in Turkey. "This is what America and the West needs to understand," complains an AK official. America also relies heavily on Turkey for its operations in Iraq. The Incirlik airbase in southern Turkey is a supply hub for American troops in Iraq and Afghanistan. As it begins to withdraw from Iraq, America is turning to Turkey to help Iraqis rebuild.

Indeed, Mr Erdogan may have a harder task explaining to Mr Obama his reluctance to back new sanctions against Iran. Turkey holds a rotating seat on the UN Security Council. "Should sanctions come to a vote, that is when we will know whose side Turkey is on: ours or the other," comments a Western diplomat. Iran will be critical for future relations with America.

Mr Erdogan's enemies claim that AK's moves to trim the army's powers are not to do with its European Union aspirations but with a desire to cement religious rule. The Ergenekon case against alleged coup-plotters was, they argue, cooked up as part of this plan. Their views have been echoed in some Western newspapers, which have also condemned a crushing tax slapped on Turkey's largest media conglomerate, Dogan. Many note that the fine came only after some Dogan titles began exposing corruption implicating AK party officials. The argument is that Mr Erdogan wants to silence a free press to help Turkey's move towards Islamic dictatorship.

Mr Erdogan undoubtedly has autocratic instincts. He has taken journalists and even cartoonists to court. His embrace of Sudan's president Omar al-Bashir, charged with war crimes against his own people, was a disgrace. And he favours a somewhat greater role for Islam in public life. But he seems committed to Turkey's EU accession process, even to pursuing liberalising reforms in Turkey if its EU hopes are dashed. He wants to resolve Turkey's problems with its Kurds. And he is pursuing reconciliation with Armenia. These are hardly signs of a shift from the West.

And what of his opponents? Deniz Baykal, the leader of the Republican People's Party, spends most of his time attacking laws that could help Turkey's bid for EU membership. Devlet Bahceli, the leader of the main nationalist party, said that "swine flu doesn't exist", though it has killed almost 200 Turks. As for the army, incriminating documents that were seized during an investigation show that a group was indeed hoping to topple Mr Erdogan by, among other things, assassinating Christians and placing the blame on AK. Why not send them to Afghanistan?

The Status of U.S. Nuclear Weapons in Turkey[*]

By Alexandra Bell and Benjamin Loehrke
Bulletin of the Atomic Scientists, November 23, 2009

For more than 40 years, Turkey has been a quiet custodian of U.S. tactical nuclear weapons. During the Cold War, Washington positioned intermediate-range nuclear missiles and bombers there to serve as a bulwark against the Soviet Union (i.e., to defend the region against Soviet attack and to influence Soviet strategic calculations). In the event of a Soviet assault on Europe, the weapons were to be fired as one of the first retaliatory shots. But as the Cold War waned, so, too, did the weapons' strategic value. Thus, over the last few decades, the United States has removed all of its intermediate-range missiles from Turkey and reduced its other nuclear weapons there through gradual redeployments and arms control agreements.

Today, Turkey hosts an estimated 90 B61 gravity bombs at Incirlik Air Base. Fifty of these bombs are reportedly assigned for delivery by U.S. pilots, and forty are assigned for delivery by the Turkish Air Force. However, no permanent nuclear-capable U.S. fighter wing is based at Incirlik, and the Turkish Air Force is reportedly not certified for NATO nuclear missions, meaning nuclear-capable F-16s from other U.S. bases would need to be brought in if Turkey's bombs were ever needed.

Such a relaxed posture makes clear just how little NATO relies on tactical nuclear weapons for its defense anymore. In fact, the readiness of NATO's nuclear forces now is measured in months as opposed to hours or days. Supposedly, the weapons are still deployed as a matter of deterrence, but the crux of deterrence is sustaining an aggressor's perception of guaranteed rapid reprisal—a perception the nuclear bombs deployed in Turkey cannot significantly add to because they are unable to be rapidly launched. Aggressors are more likely to be deterred by NATO's conventional power or the larger strategic forces supporting its nuclear umbrella.

So in effect, U.S. tactical nuclear weapons in Turkey are without military value or purpose. That means removing them from the country should be simple, right? Unfortunately, matters of national and international security are never that easy.

Roadblocks to removal. In 2005, when NATO's top commander at the time, Gen. James L. Jones, supported the elimination of U.S. nuclear weapons in Europe, he was met with fierce political resistance. (In addition to the 90 B61 bombs in Turkey, there are another 110 or so U.S. bombs located at bases in Belgium, Germany, Italy, and the Netherlands.) Four years later, some U.S. and European officials still maintain that the political value of the nuclear weapons is enough to keep them deployed across Europe. In particular, they argue that the weapons are "an essential political and military link" between NATO members and help maintain alliance cohesion. The Defense Department's 2008 report on nuclear weapons management concurred: "As long as our allies value [the nuclear weapons'] political contribution, the United States is obligated to provide and maintain the nuclear weapon capability."

Those who hold this view believe that nuclear sharing is both symbolic of alliance cohesion and a demonstration of how the United States and NATO have committed to defending each other in the event of an attack. They argue that removing the weapons would dangerously undermine such cohesion and raise questions about how committed Washington is to its NATO allies.

But NATO's post-Cold War struggles with cohesion are a result of far more than disagreement over tactical nuclear deployments. NATO has given Turkey plenty of reasons to doubt its members' commitment to Ankara on several recent occasions. For example, before both Iraq wars, some NATO members hesitated to provide Turkey with air defenses or to assist it with displaced persons who had fled into its territory. Moreover, Turkey, which values NATO as a direct connection to Washington, witnessed the United States completely ignore its vehement opposition to the most recent Iraq War. Additionally, Ankara is dismayed by the reluctance of some of its NATO allies to label the Kurdistan Workers' Party, which has caused violent chaos along the Turkish border, as a terrorist organization.

Then there is the issue of Tehran's nuclear program, which seriously complicates any discussion of the United States removing its tactical nuclear weapons from Turkey. An Iranian nuclear capability could spark an arms race in the Middle East and bring about a "proliferation cascade," which could cause Turkey to reconsider its nuclear options—especially if the United States pulls its nuclear weapons from Incirlik. When asked directly about its response to an Iranian nuclear weapon, a high-ranking Foreign Ministry official said that Turkey would immediately arm itself with a bomb. This isn't Ankara's official policy, but it seems to indicate a general feeling among its leaders. Whether Turkey is primarily concerned about security or prestige, the bottom line is that it would not sit idly by as Iran established a regional hegemony.

A prescription for withdrawal. Preventing Turkey (and any other country in the region) from acquiring nuclear weapons is critical to international security. Doing so requires a key factor that also is essential to paving the way toward withdrawal of U.S. nuclear weapons: improved alliance relations. The political and strategic compasses are pointing to the eventual withdrawal of nuclear weapons from Europe—it's a strategy that certainly fits the disarmament agenda President Barack Obama has outlined. But to get there, careful diplomacy will be required to improve U.S.-Turkish ties and to assuage Turkish security concerns.

The U.S.-Turkish relationship cooled when Turkey refused to participate in Operation Iraqi Freedom, after which Turkish support for U.S. policy declined through the end of the George W. Bush administration. Obama's election has helped to mend fences, and his visit to Turkey in April was warmly received. In fact, all of the administration's positive interactions with Turkey have been beneficial: Washington has supported Turkey's role as a regional energy supplier and encouraged Ankara as it undertakes difficult political reforms and works to resolve regional diplomatic conflicts. For its part, Turkey recently doubled its troop contribution to NATO's Security Assistance Force in Afghanistan—a boon to U.S. efforts there.

By incorporating Ankara into its new European missile defense plans—intended to protect Turkey and other countries vulnerable to Iran's short- and intermediate-range ballistic missiles—Washington could further shore up its military relationship with Turkey. Ship-based Aegis missile systems will be the backbone of the strategy, with considerations left open for later deployments of mobile ground-based interceptors in Eastern Europe or Turkey. This cooperation could provide the bond with Washington and perception of security that Turkey seeks in the face of a potential Iranian bomb.

Because Russia weighs significantly in Turkish security calculations, reductions to Russian strategic and nonstrategic nuclear arsenals also would help improve Ankara's peace of mind. The United States and Russia soon will seek ratification of a follow-on agreement to START. And treaty negotiations in pursuit of further reductions to the U.S. and Russian arsenals should involve forward-deployed nuclear weapons, including the U.S. weapons in Turkey. During any such negotiations, Turkey must be fully confident in NATO and U.S. security guarantees. Critically, any removal of the weapons in Turkey would need to happen in concert with efforts to prevent Iran from turning its civil nuclear energy program into a military one. Otherwise, Washington would risk compromising Turkey as a NATO ally and key regional partner.

If used properly, Turkey actually can play an important role in this complex process, and the United States and its allies should seriously consider

Turkish offers to serve as an interlocutor between Iran and the West. First, Ankara's potential influence with Tehran should not be underestimated. As Princeton scholar Joshua Walker has noted, given its long-established pragmatic relations and growing economic ties with Iran, Ankara is in a position to positively influence Tehran's behavior.

More largely, if the United States and European Union task Turkey with a bigger role in the diplomatic back-and-forth with Iran, it would help convince Ankara (and others) of Turkey's value to NATO and have the additional benefit of pulling Ankara into a closer relationship with Washington and Brussels. As a result, Turkey would obtain a stronger footing in alliance politics, contain its chief security concerns, and foster the necessary conditions for the removal of tactical U.S. nuclear weapons from Turkish soil.

Unwelcomed Missiles[*]

Feryaz Ocakli and Yelena Biberman
RIA Novosti Russia Profile, December 29, 2009

In the latest chapter of the U.S. missile defense system (MDS) saga, Turkey has rejected U.S. President Barack Obama's proposal to deploy missile shield elements on its soil for fear of Russian retaliation. The twist is that it was Russian President Vladimir Putin who, back in June 2007, suggested Turkey as an alternative site for MDS interceptors. It is unclear whether Russia serves as an excuse or the real reason for Turkey's reluctance to get into the MDS business. In other words, it is unclear who is wagging Washington: Moscow or Ankara? The answer is—both.

This is not the first time Ankara is involved in a missile dispute between Washington and Moscow. The escalation of events that ultimately led to the 1962 Cuban Missile Crisis began in Turkey. Missiles stationed there boosted American nuclear capabilities at the expense of the Soviet Union. Only when Moscow responded in kind by attempting to install its own nuclear missiles in Cuba did Washington agree to dismantle its arsenal in Turkey.

The George W. Bush administration proposed to install the MDS in Poland and the Czech Republic in 2007. The White House declared that the missile defense system would help to counter a possible Iranian missile threat. The Kremlin responded by signaling that it would station short-range Iskander missiles in Kaliningrad, a Russian exclave bordering Poland, and accused the White House of using Cold War tactics against a rejuvenating Russia. Putin hinted at Turkey, Iraq, and Israel as potential, non-threatening locations for the defense system instead of Russia's western border with the European Union. When the Obama administration decided to drop Warsaw and Prague off the agenda, Washington returned to Ankara.

Obama first voiced the possibility of installing the MDS in Turkey during Turkish Prime Minister Recep Tayyip Erdogan's visit to Washington on December 7. Turkish daily *Milliyet* soon quoted a Turkish military source claiming: 'both Russia and Iran [would] perceive that as a threat.' Several days before Erdogan's Washington trip, Russia's ambassador to Ankara Vladimir Ivanovskiy told Turkish daily *Aksam* that Russia would approve of an MDS in Turkey if Turkey, the United States and Russia act as 'partners' to the project. Why, then, is Ankara turning down Washington's request?

The first plausible explanation for Turkey's puzzling behavior is that it is an attempt to please Russia by helping it get a larger role in the missile defense project. After all, Russia is Turkey's largest trading partner, and Turkey depends on Russia for 65 percent of its natural gas and 40 percent of its oil imports. There are some signs that the United States is at least considering bringing Russia into the project, at least as long as Iran remains the bigger threat. NATO's new Secretary General Anders Fogh Rasmussen called for 'linking the United States, NATO and Russia missile defense systems at an appropriate time.' Associated Press reported Russian envoy Dmitry Rogozin responding by calling cooperation with Russia 'not a matter of choice but of necessity.'

The second explanation lies in Turkey's recent shift in foreign policy. Since the Turkish Parliament rejected the Bush administration's plan to open a northern front in the invasion of Iraq in 2003, Turkey has increasingly asserted itself as a diplomatic force in the Middle East, Eastern Europe, and the Southern Caucasus. Ankara has turned to a policy of 'zero problems' with its neighbors. Surrounded by countries historically seen as rivals at best, Turkey has traditionally oriented itself towards the United States and Western Europe at the expense of closer relations with its neighbors.

Still, Turkey's recent shift in foreign policy should not be confused with a turn away from 'the West.' Ankara misses no opportunity to reassert its intentions to join the European Union, and to remain a 'strategic partner' to the United States, even when the latter seems less than enthusiastic to establish the relationship as such. Turkey's new foreign minister, Ahmet Davutoglu, symbolizes the shift in policy orientation. As a chief advisor to the prime minister before his new appointment, he is credited with masterminding Turkey's shift toward the 'zero problems with neighbors' approach.

Ankara's unwillingness to accept Washington's missiles on Turkish soil reflects Turkey's new foreign policy line. While striving to maintain its close strategic ties with the United States, Turkey is also juggling newly improved relations with Moscow and Tehran. Iran is Turkey's second biggest supplier of gas and oil, after Russia, and trade between the two countries is steadily increasing. Ankara is also taking a cautious approach toward Iran's nuclear program, frequently voicing its disapproval of sanctions against Tehran.

Moreover, Ankara is concerned about becoming a front against Iran. Installation of an American MDS in Turkey would inherently be perceived as an offensive move by Tehran, and Turkey wants to avoid becoming a target for Iranian missiles—a possible byproduct of a defense system intended to improve security against this threat. On the other hand, Turkey is considering acquiring its own MDS from either the United States, Russia, or China. The details of this purchase have yet to be worked out.

As the issue stands today, Turkey will not want to take part in a future standoff between neither Washington and Tehran nor Washington and Moscow. The United States would therefore find it difficult to compel Turkey to redefine its foreign policy in a way that would directly compromise Ankara's relations with its neighbors and, especially, Russia.

5

Japan: From Article 9 to "Yankee Go Home!"

Editor's Introduction

In August 1945 the United States dropped atomic bombs on the Japanese cities of Hiroshima and Nagasaki, instantly killing tens of thousands of people and exposing many more to deadly radiation. While other nations emerged from World War II having suffered higher casualty rates, Japan was the lone belligerent to experience firsthand the horror of nuclear warfare. The bombings hastened the country's surrender, and two years later, as the Diet, or parliament, drew up Japan's postwar constitution, it took a staunchly pacifistic stance. "Aspiring sincerely to an international peace based on justice and order, the Japanese people forever renounce war as a sovereign right of the nation and the threat or use of force as means of settling international disputes," read Article 9, which prohibited Japan from establishing any offensive military capability.

In the early 1950s, as communists fought for control of Korea, receiving support from China and the Soviet Union, Japan and the United States realized there was much to be gained by an East Asian military partnership. The nations signed the Mutual Security Treaty and Mutual Defense Assistance Agreement, treaties that established an alliance that has lasted more than a half-century. In exchange for agreeing to protect Japan, both with conventional and nuclear weapons, the U.S. military gained a toehold in the vital region, establishing a string of permanent bases.

The articles in this chapter trace the history of post-war U.S.-Japanese relations and consider whether arrangements made during the Cold War remain at all relevant. In the first selection, "U.S. Forces: Basics of the U.S. Military Presence," Reiji Yoshida answers questions from readers concerning the alliance. Several of the queries center on recent controversies, among them charges U.S. troops accused of crimes receive unfair legal privileges.

In "The New Battle of Okinawa: America's Security Treaty With Japan," a contributor to *The Economist* examines the controversy surrounding the Futenma Marine Corps Air Station, a base many residents of Okinawa, the Japanese island that houses the bulk of U.S. forces, would like to see moved elsewhere. In the wake of frequent noise complaints and a 1995 incident in which three American servicemen raped a 12-year-old Japanese girl, U.S. officials agreed in 2006 to move the base to a less populated area of Okinawa.

Newly elected Prime Minister Yukio Hatoyama has since called for a review of that plan, creating a political stalemate that, as of this writing, has yet to be resolved.

In the next article, "Is Defence Treaty With US Set to Collapse?" David McNeill moves from the controversy in Okinawa to the larger question of whether the U.S.-Japanese military partnership could be drawing to a close. McNeill calls the alliance "one of the odder creations of international diplomacy," since it requires Japan, a purportedly nonviolent nation, to support the United States' various global military campaigns. While some have urged Hatoyama to sever ties and set Japan on a path toward military self-reliance, others worry that doing so would yield unpleasant consequences, such as huge spikes in defense spending.

With "Japan Balks at $2 Billion Bill to Host U.S. Troops," the next selection, Associated Press writer Eric Talmadge examines the debate over who should pay to house, feed, and entertain U.S. troops stationed in Japan. As it stands, the host nation spends more than $2 billion a year to support U.S. forces. Some Japanese citizens, particularly those Okinawans who live near the golf course at Kadena Air Base, feel this amount is too high.

In "A Changed Japanese Diplomacy?" Anthony Rowley looks at how the Hatoyama administration's desire to strengthen ties with China and other Asian countries could further strain relations with the United States and weaken the military alliance.

Karen Sue Smith wonders whether Japan, in assisting the United States with its War on Terror, is contradicting its pacifist principles in "The Power of Japan," the final selection in this chapter. "The questions facing Japan are serious," Smith writes. "Can Japan remain dependent upon the United States and willfully unable to protect itself, even as more large or unstable nations nearby acquire nuclear weapons?"

U.S. Forces*

Basics of the U.S. Military Presence

By Reiji Yoshida
The Japan Times, March 25, 2008

The issue of U.S. military forces in Japan has come to the fore again following the alleged rape of a 14-year-old Okinawan girl by a U.S. Marine. Although the girl has withdrawn the accusation, locals and politicians have seized on the incident— a reminder of the 1995 gang rape of a 12-year-old girl by two marines and a navy corpsman—to compel a rethink of the presence of U.S. forces in Japan.

Following are some questions and answers on the matter:

How many U.S. service members are based in Japan, how many dependents do they have with them here and what is the breakdown by branch of service?

According to U.S. Forces Japan headquarters at Yokota Air Base, as of February there were 47,200 service members based in Japan, including 11,700 aboard vessels of the 7th Fleet. In addition, there were 3,510 U.S. civilian personnel and 41,695 family members. Of the 47,200 service members, 17,400 were in the navy, 15,000 in the marines corps, 12,300 in the air force and 2,500 in the army.

Okinawa hosts more service members by far than any other prefecture. According to the prefectural government, Okinawa was home to 23,140 U.S. military-related individuals, including 13,480 marines and 7,080 airmen, as of September 2006.

How much land do U.S. bases in Japan occupy?

As of March 2006, the 87 facilities exclusively used by the U.S. military covered an area roughly half the size of the 23 wards of Tokyo, or 312.2 sq. km.

Yet Okinawa, which makes up only 0.6 percent of the nation's land area, contributes 74.7 percent of the land for the bases.

Who are the owners of the vast compounds exclusively used by the U.S. forces?

On the mainland, most of the land where U.S. bases are located belongs to the Japanese government and other public entities and is provided free of charge, based on the Japan-U.S. Security Treaty.

The treaty obliges Japan to give the U.S. use of those properties to maintain peace and order in Japan and the Far East. Many such compounds on the mainland were formerly owned and used by the Imperial Japanese Army and Navy.

In contrast, in Okinawa one-third of the area used by U.S. forces is privately owned, most of it having been confiscated by the U.S. military soon after the war. The U.S. occupied Okinawa until its reversion in 1972 despite Japan's recovery of independence with the 1951 San Francisco Treaty.

Today, the Japanese government pays a considerable amount of rent to the landowners.

Why were U.S. troops initially stationed in Japan?

The U.S. military in Japan traces its origin to the postwar Occupation, beginning with the arrival of Gen. Douglas MacArthur at Atsugi airfield in Kanagawa Prefecture as Supreme Allied Commander on Aug. 30, 1945.

The outbreak of the Korean War in 1950 made Japan an important strategic base for the U.S. during the Cold War confrontation, which prompted the two countries to conclude the bilateral security treaty maintaining U.S. forces in Japan.

What are the strategic benefits for the U.S. of stationing forces in Japan today?

Experts say U.S. bases in Japan are extremely important for the U.S. to maintain its military presence in the Asia-Pacific region and beyond, even as far as the Indian Ocean and Persian Gulf. For example, the Yokosuka Naval Base in Kanagawa Prefecture is often described as the most strategically important U.S. naval installation overseas.

Similarly, Okinawa, because of its proximity to the Taiwan Strait as well as mainland China and the Korean Peninsula, has been dubbed by the U.S. military "The Keystone of the Pacific."

Many military vessels, airplanes and service members, including the aircraft carrier USS Kitty Hawk, Aegis destroyers, F-15 fighters and marine corps units, have been dispatched from bases in Japan to fight in Iraq and maintain postwar security operations there.

The recent alleged rape in Okinawa prompted opposition parties and 14 prefectural governors to launch separate calls for a revision of the Status of Forces Agreement. What is the SOFA?

When a country allows U.S. forces to be stationed on its territory in peacetime, the two countries usually conclude a Status of Forces Agreement to define the legal status of the military personnel. Without such an agreement, conflicts may occur between the legal authorities of the two countries over such matters as immigration, tax and customs and criminal and civil jurisdiction. Japan and the U.S. signed a SOFA in 1960.

Is it true, as critics charge, that the SOFA gives unfair privileges to the U.S. forces here?

Japanese local leaders and antimilitary activists often criticize the SOFA for giving virtual extraterritorial rights to U.S. personnel.

In particular, they point out that under the accord, criminal suspects with the U.S. military are held on U.S. bases in the custody of U.S. forces, and are handed over to Japanese authorities only after an indictment is filed.

The Foreign Ministry, however, argues that the SOFA is not unfair, and in fact gives more favorable conditions to the Japanese side than most other SOFAs the U.S. has concluded with other countries.

For example, under the U.S. SOFA with Germany, U.S. military suspects are handed over to the German side only when punishment is actually meted out against convicted criminals, not at the time of indictment as under the Japan-U.S. SOFA.

How much support, both direct and indirect, does Japan provide to help shoulder the cost of the U.S. forces in Japan?

According to a 2004 report by the U.S. Department of Defense, Japan contributed direct financial support worth $3.23 billion and indirect support worth $1.18 billion in fiscal 2002, which offset as much as 74.5 percent of the total costs for the U.S. to station its forces in Japan.

"Japan . . . provides over $4 billion in host-nation support—the most generous of any U.S. ally—and remains steadfast in supporting its share of the costs of alliance transformation," Adm. Timothy Keating, naval commander of the U.S. Pacific Command, testified before the Senate Armed Services Committee on March 11.

Japan's direct financial support includes paying the salaries of some 25,000 nonmilitary workers at U.S. military facilities in Japan. Japan also pays for the electricity, gas, water and sewage as well as for the cooking and heating fuels at U.S. military housing facilities.

The New Battle of Okinawa[*]

Wrangling Over an American Base Puts Japan's New Government in a Bind

The Economist, January 16, 2010

On the wall of the Sakima Art Museum in this bustling city [Ginowan City, Japan] is a work called the Battle of Okinawa. It depicts the suffering of local civilians during the American invasion of Okinawa in 1945, partly at the hands of murderous-looking Japanese troops. On the roof of the museum, there is a more mischievous—but equally effective—work of anti-war polemic, this time directed against the Americans. A platform looks out over the fenced-off Futenma Marine Corps Air Station, which stretches out to the sea over an area larger than Central Park in New York. In just a few minutes, your correspondent witnessed a transport plane taking off, three fighter jets roaring overhead and a military helicopter rumbling to life. An aircraft-carrier might be less noisy.

The base was seized by the American army in 1945, but since then Ginowan has grown to surround it with offices, homes and government buildings. Ginowan is only a small city, of 92,000 people; even so, imagine how New Yorkers living around Central Park would feel, were it an air base bristling with marines belonging to a country that once colonised them. That gives a sense of why Futenma, however much it has helped keep the peace in East Asia, has long needed to move.

That much America and Japan agree upon. Negotiations to find a replacement have dragged on since 1996, the year after three American marines gang-raped a 12-year-old Okinawan girl. But since the Democratic Party of Japan (DPJ) took power last September, the issue has opened an unusually deep wound in relations between the two countries. It still festers. On January 12th Katsuya Okada, Japan's foreign minister, and Hillary Clinton,

America's secretary of state, agreed not to let the dispute stop them discussing other ways to bolster their military alliance. But Mrs Clinton continued to press for Futenma to be relocated in Okinawa.

The friction is partly to be expected. In opposition the DPJ repeatedly objected to an agreement to move part of the air station, including landing strips, to a pristine bay in north-eastern Okinawa, in exchange for the withdrawal of 8,000 marines and their families to American territory in Guam. Yukio Hatoyama, the new prime minister, personally promised Okinawans during the election campaign that Futenma would be shunted off the island.

That promise swiftly put his government at loggerheads with the Obama administration. As one of her first acts of diplomacy last February, Mrs Clinton signed an agreement under which Japan would contribute $6 billion to relocating Futenma. The other signatory was from the former Liberal Democratic government, which was doomed to suffer an electoral rout in August. But a deal, the Obama administration insisted to the DPJ, was a deal. Some analysts believe that may have been an overly bossy assessment. Even under the Liberal Democratic Party (LDP), which for much of its 53 years in power was a pliant American ally, the Futenma relocation was often a source of friction.

Indeed, over the decades relations with the LDP had not always been smooth. They got off to a good start. The 1960 Treaty of Mutual Co-operation and Security turned out to be a strikingly successful insurance policy. The Japanese paid the premiums by offering American troops bases and cash. The Americans promised nuclear and non-nuclear American deterrence, which helped underwrite peace in the region, while at the same time acting as a "cork in the bottle" against possible Japanese remilitarisation.

But after the cold war relations appeared to come adrift. When Junichiro Koizumi, prime minister from 2001–06, pledged strong support for the "war on terror" after September 11, 2001, America hoped Japan would take on a global security role commensurate with its economic power. But it did not. According to a recent study by Michael Finnegan of the National Bureau of Asian Research, a think-tank in Seattle, America and Japan no longer see eye-to-eye on "what constitutes a threat to their shared interests." Both countries still refer to the alliance as a cornerstone of their security policies, but it is, says Mr Finnegan, a brittle one.

Defenders of the alliance argue that it has done more than keep the peace: it has enabled Japan to keep its military spending low, and attract global status in other ways, notably economic. Nonetheless, some in Japan feel the country has subordinated itself to America, and this has riled nationalists. And in Washington, DC, critics accuse Japan of "cheap-riding" on American security guarantees.

It is against this backdrop that the new government's review of the Futenma accord raised hackles in Washington. Adding to the sense of drift was Tokyo's decision to end an eight-year maritime refuelling mission for troops fighting in Afghanistan this month. It has also promised to investigate secret agreements in the 1960s and 1970s that enabled nuclear-armed American warships to enter Japan.

Above all, since the DPJ took power, it has been unclear how its goal of partially balancing Japan's ties to America with closer ones to China would affect the American alliance. The 50th anniversary of the security treaty might be a good chance to update the accord to reflect China's rise. But security analysts say the Futenma dispute threatens the mutual trust needed for such an undertaking.

PAYBACK TIME

To make matters worse, most Okinawans seem determined to hold Mr Hatoyama to his word about removing the base altogether. As the painting at the Sakima gallery suggests, Okinawa nurtures an historic grudge against the mother country, piqued by the second world war massacre. Many locals feel that for too long Tokyo has outsourced American bases to the island—it houses 60% of American forces and their families in Japan—and offered only grubby fiscal handouts in return.

Critics accuse the Japanese authorities of producing a cooked-up environmental assessment, which skates over the dangers the new base would pose to the dugong, a rare sea mammal that grazes on sea grasses near the site of the proposed airstrips. Even supporters of the new base admit that it is hard to judge the full ecological impact because America has given imprecise figures about how many troops and aircraft would remain.

If the Hatoyama administration does break its promise to the Okinawans, it would be "suicidal," says Yoichi Iha, mayor of Ginowan and a staunch opponent of the agreement. And even then, some fear that protesters could make it very difficult to start construction work. A mayoral election takes place on January 24th in Nago, the city where the new base is proposed. Relocation is the main campaign issue. If the incumbent who supports it is ousted, that will be a strong indication of the level of anger. An election for governor of Okinawa in November is likely to bring the same tensions to the fore island-wide. But with America sticking to its guns, the Hatoyama administration is bound to upset one side or other. Its battle of Okinawa has only just begun.

Is Defence Treaty with US Set to Collapse?*

By David McNeill
The Irish Times, February 15, 2010

Almost exactly half a century ago, Tokyo and Washington signed a land-mark agreement so divisive it forced then US president Dwight D Eisen-hower to cancel a trip to Japan, led to the resignation of Japan's prime minister Nobusuke Kishi and sparked large riots and violent demonstrations by students and trade unionists across the country.

Yet, despite the best efforts of its opponents, the US-Japan Security Treaty (Ampo)—the keystone of US defence policy in Asia—is still with us. The two sides officially celebrated its anniversary last month, even as they were buffeted by what could be the most serious crisis in the treaty's history. Many wonder if it will survive 2010 at all.

The treaty is one of the odder creations of international diplomacy because it depends on a key contradiction: how can a country that is supposedly neutral and pacifist also be a key player in the American global defence network? The answer, points out Japan-based political scientist Douglas Lummis, is Okinawa, Japan's southern-most prefecture.

Nearly 1,000 miles from Tokyo, and a psychological world away, Okinawa hosts about 75 per cent of all US military facilities in Japan. Thousands of young marines—many battle-scarred from Iraq and Afghanistan—are uneasily stationed there. The marine's Futenma air base squats right in the centre of crowded Ginowan city, bringing noise, pollution and crime.

For decades, Okinawans complained of being forced to bear the burdens—and contradictions—of the nation's entire defence strategy. Out of sight and mostly out of mind of the mainland, they demanded the US bases and troops be spread more evenly in Japan. Until last year, they were largely ignored by a succession of conservative governments led by the Liberal Democrats (LDP). But the election of the liberal-left Democrats (DPJ) under prime minister Yukio Hatoyama has raised expectations of long-awaited change.

The prime minister has made little secret of his desire to end what he calls Japan's "subservience" to US interests. He has publicly questioned whether Japan should host any American troops during peacetime and called for a major reassessment of a defence strategy he believes is still frozen in cold war amber.

Before being elected, he demanded a review of a 2006 agreement calling for the relocation of the ageing Futenma base to a pristine, ecologically important area off Okinawa's northern coastline. Okinawans responded by overwhelmingly backing the Democrats in last August's general election. Now they're wondering if they made a mistake.

Caught between Washington's increasingly insistent demands to honour the 2006 deal and his promise to Okinawa, Hatoyama dithered before deciding to appoint a government committee to adjudicate. His strategy now seems to be to wait until the outcome of local elections in Okinawa before making a final decision in May.

In the meantime, the prospect of having to live beside a huge new US airbase has alarmed the citizens of Nago, the nearest small city. Local polls show opposition running at over well over 70 per cent. Last month, voters opted for anti-base candidate Susumu Inamine against Yoshikazu Shimabukuro, who said the facility would bring jobs and money to the local economy.

Inamine has added heft to a campaign largely shouldered until now by pensioners and students, who have camped for years in Heneko, the village that will host the US facility. The election outcome has added a layer of complexity: "National security policy cannot be made in towns and villages," Lieut Gen Keith J Stalder, commander of marine forces in the Pacific, said last month.

Pressure is coming too from Hatoyama's domestic opponents, who say he risks badly damaging the half-century alliance and has not seriously considered the implications of unhitching Japan's defence wagon from its US partner. Opting for the Hatoyama route means Japan "would have to increase its five trillion yen defence budget by 10 per cent annually for the next 10 years," warned *Sentaku* political magazine this month.

As the deadline for a decision nears, many analysts believe Hatoyama will give way to US demands and face down the Okinawans—probably the least worst political option. But many have been surprised by his stubbornness. Whatever the final outcome of the dispute, says veteran Japan watcher Gavan McCormack in an essay in *Japan Focus*, "the Hatoyama government has so far withstood the most sustained barrage of US pressure, intimidation, insult, ultimatum, and threat, and decided, at least for the present, to say: 'No.'"

Japan Balks at $2 Billion Bill to Host U.S. Troops*

By Eric Talmadge
The Associated Press, February 7, 2010

In a country where land is a precious commodity, many U.S. military bases in Japan boast golf courses, football fields and shopping malls whose food courts offer everything from Subway and Starbucks.

They are the most visible point of grievance in a sharpening debate about the cost to Japan—about $2 billion a year—of supporting the 47,000 American service members here. That's about three times what Germany pays to host U.S. forces on its soil.

But facing economic woes and seeking a more equal relationship with the U.S., Japan's new reformist government is questioning whether it should spend so much on U.S. troops—a topic that was taboo under the pro-Washington administrations that governed Japan for most of the post-World War II era.

American officials say the deployment in Japan of troops, fighter jets and the only nuclear-powered aircraft carrier based outside the U.S. has enabled Japan to hold down its own defense costs in line with its pacifist constitution. They also say the U.S. presence prevents an arms race in east Asia, acts as a deterrent against North Korea and counters the rise of China.

Japan covers much of the cost for supporting American troops, including utilities, maintenance and physical upgrades plus the wages of tens of thousands of Japanese civilians working on the bases.

The scrutiny in Japan, Washington's deep-pocketed ally and most important strategic partner in Asia, comes as the U.S. defense budget is focused on Iraq and Afghanistan. The Japanese call their share a "kindness budget," implying the U.S. is getting a free ride, and its opponents say it is rife with waste.

The flash point of the debate is the southern island of Okinawa, where most of the nearly 100 U.S. facilities in Japan are located.

Futenma airfield, where several thousand Marines are stationed, was to have been moved from the town of Ginowan to Nago, on a less crowded part of the island. But that plan came into doubt last month after Nago elected a mayor who opposes having the base.

At the same time, the U.S. is shifting about 8,000 troops from Okinawa to the U.S. territory of Guam and expects Japan to pay an estimated $6 billion of the moving costs.

The frustrations run deep in cramped Ginowan. Local media regularly run images of the golf course at nearby Kadena Air Base and criticize the forces relentlessly whenever a service member is involved in a local crime.

"When people who live in crowded areas in small houses drive by and see the situation on the bases, some feel angry," said Hideki Toma, an official dealing with the bases on Okinawa.

"This is a bigger issue than the golf courses and free highway passes," Toma said. "It goes back to the fact that Okinawa was occupied after World War II and why the bases have to be here in the first place."

That sentiment is widely shared, and it underscores a feeling that the bases should be spread out more evenly among Japan's main islands and Okinawa. Okinawa was one of the bloodiest battlefields of World War II, and Okinawans feel that the continued U.S. presence places an uneven burden on them, though the argument that all U.S. forces should leave Japan is not popular.

Facilities such as on-base golf courses represent a fraction of the sum U.S. taxpayers chip in for the defense of Japan—about $3.9 billion a year, according to a State Department official who spoke on condition of anonymity because he was not authorized to discuss the details.

"There is no difference in the facilities that our forces have here than they have anywhere else in the world, including the United States," Lt. Gen. Benjamin Mixon, the commander of the U.S Army's Pacific Forces, told The Associated Press. "But we cannot view forces that are out here simply as Japan. They are in Asia; they are available for responsive deployment."

Eiichi Hoshino, professor of international relations at the University of the Ryukyus, said previous governments were too willing to pay because they wanted to maintain a special relationship with the United States.

"If the United States wants to stay here at any cost, it should be the one who is paying," he said.

Tokyo's share rose sharply until 2001 but has since decreased steadily, largely because of the shrinking economy and the objections of Yukio Hatoyama's Democratic Party when it was in the opposition. Costs have been cut, in part, by reducing utilities payments and the salaries and number of Japanese base employees, a process members of Hatoyama's party want to accelerate now that he is prime minister.

He says the alliance with the U.S. remains a keystone of Japanese policy, but he wants to re-evaluate it. "This will be a very important year for our relationship," Hatoyama said last month.

A Changed Japanese Diplomacy?[*]

By Anthony Rowley
Business Times Singapore, November 14, 2009

"Go Home Yankee" is not a slogan that I can recall being uttered, publicly at least, in the near 20 years that I have lived in Japan—until this week that is. Admittedly, it was used not by a Japanese, but by a foreign journalist questioning an Okinawa assemblyman about continuation of the US military presence in Japan. The response from the Japanese lawmaker was revealing however.

It suggested that the writing (if not yet 'go home' graffiti) may be on the wall and that the presence of the US military in parts of Asia, Japan especially, is being questioned as the new government of Prime Minister Yukio Hatoyama seeks closer ties with East Asia and a "more equal" relationship with the United States.

"Our movement is not going international yet," said Yonekichi Shinzato, a member of the Okinawa prefectural assembly and one of a group of public officials who want the US Marines out of their island. But he and others are "in touch with citizen movements" in places as far afield as South Korea, the Philippines and Puerto Rico, said the assemblyman.

"Some nations have been able to get US bases out of their country" by popular protest, as in the Philippines where a formerly 'huge' US military presence was ended by such means, added Shinzato, rather politely, after being asked whether Okinawa is yet ready to say "Yankee Go Home" rather than simply calling for a diminished US military presence there.

The assemblyman shared a platform this week with the mayors of two Okinawa cities—Yoichi Iha from Ginowan and Takeshi Onaga from Naha—during a debate at the Foreign Correspondents Club of Japan in Tokyo this week.

Their immediate demands, which they urged Hatoyama to put to US President Barack Obama when he comes to Tokyo yesterday, are very specific.

* Source: The Business Times © Singapore Press Holdings Limited. Reprinted with permission.

These relate to the US Marines' Futenma air base in Okinawa, which they say is "the most dangerous in the world" and want closed, and to the proposed new Henoko base, which they want scrapped.

Feelings are running high in Japan's southernmost island over these issues. "Okinawa prefecture was made a battlefield for ground war in the (Second) World War," said a statement distributed by the three emissaries who came to Tokyo to present their case prior to Obama's visit.

"After the War, (our) abundant land was taken away by the bayonets and bulldozers of the US Army and put under army occupation," said the statement issued following a mass rally in Okinawa on Nov 8. Some 37 years have passed since Okinawa was returned to Japan by the US, but still it has to host 75 per cent of the special facilities for the US Army in Japan, it added.

Okinawa residents have been emboldened by the stance taken by Hatoyama over where the Futenma base should be relocated once it is closed. He has refused to bow to pressure for a quick decision, despite "seemingly threatening" attempts (as the statement put it) by US Defense Secretary Robert Gates to secure a quick decision from Tokyo.

What is at stake is more than the logistics of where US forces in Japan are located: It is the fundamental issue of Japan's relationship with the US and with its Asian neighbours. Under the Liberal Democratic Party that ruled Japan for half a century until a few months ago, it was assumed that Japan would host US forces in return for security and access to the US market.

OKINAWA ISSUE

The Okinawa issue has become what assemblyman Shinzato called a 'touchstone' of future relations between Japan and the US, but it is not the only one. Mr Hatoyama's decision not to renew Japan's refuelling mission for US vessels in the Indian Ocean and to modify Japan's Afghanistan mission are other examples of his desire for a changed Japanese diplomacy.

The LDP wanted Japan to exert more independence by having its Self Defence Forces play a more active role around the world instead of relying upon "aid diplomacy"—financial or otherwise. But there was an assumption under the LDP that the US remained Japan's key ally, while China and North Korea as well as Russia remained potential enemies.

The Hatoyama administration seems to be making a bolder assumption, which is that if Japan stretches out the hand of friendship to China and other East Asian neighbours, these can become key allies too and that Japan will therefore not require to shelter under the US nuclear umbrella, with all the consequences that has for wider dependence upon the US.

It is a mature, and historically inevitable, approach, but it is also one that threatens to create considerable friction between Tokyo and Washington. China and other Asian nations need to make a gesture of support for the

Hatoyama initiatives rather than go on hoping to ensure their own security by relying on a balance of competing forces in the region.

It is probably not time to say "Yankee Go Home" as yet, but it is time for Asian powers, both large and small, to begin revising their ideas in line with those of the new Japanese administration and to ask whether it is reasonable (let alone mature) to go on relying on a single (and highly indebted) super-power to underwrite their security.

The Power of Japan*

Does It Lie in Military Strength or in Its Unique Witness for Peace?

By Karen Sue Smith
America, October 22, 2007

First it was "Little Boy," then "Fat Man." Sixty-two years ago, in August 1945, the United States dropped atomic bombs on Hiroshima and Nagasaki, each a Japanese city of roughly 250,000. According to estimates, a total of 150,000 Japanese were killed immediately in the two cities, and thousands more were injured or made ill by the radiation and nuclear fallout. What few people outside Japan realize is that the death toll continues to climb. In summer 2007, when Tomihisa Taue, the Mayor of Nagasaki, led the annual commemoration of the bombing at the Nagasaki Peace Park, he added more than 3,000 deaths from bomb-related radiation illness during the previous 12 months, which brought the official death toll as of 2007 to 143,124 for Nagasaki alone.

There were, of course, survivors, the hibakusha (literally "explosion-affected people") and among them the tainai hibakusha, those nestled "in their mother's womb" when the atomic bombs exploded. It is not inconsequential that the current Archbishop of Nagasaki, the Most Reverend Joseph M. Takami, is himself one of the tainai hibakusha. Speaking at Georgetown University in March 2007, Archbishop Takami noted that he had grown up personally affected by the suffering. A week after the blast, he said, "four members of my immediate family, including my grandmother and two aunts, died." He acknowledged that Japan was not merely a victim of the war, but a willing aggressor against its Asian neighbors. Yet, speaking for many Japanese people, the archbishop said that direct experience of the atomic bomb "taught us a precious lesson of nonviolence as a way of life, a conviction, a belief and a non-negotiable commitment."

Nonviolence as a way of life needs to be recast or revitalized for the current generation of Japanese, however, for Japan's "non-negotiable commitment" to peace is being tested by developments within Asia itself, on the larger world scene and by the United States government. Since the year 2000, the U.S.-Japan relationship has been changing radically in ways that have alarmed some Japanese voters, Japan's Catholic bishops and some of the country's political leaders, like the mayor of Nagasaki. As Archbishop Takami put it in his Georgetown address, "Japan is a willing partner in the U.S. global war on terror," increasingly allowing the U.S. military to use its land, air and naval facilities as Japan itself takes on an ever larger military role. Such a role stands in direct contradiction to Japan's postwar Constitution, self-understanding and foreign policy.

POST-WORLD WAR II DEVELOPMENTS

Nonviolence as a way of life, as Archbishop Takami expressed it, is relatively new in Japan's long militant history. It took root in postwar Japan, defeated and occupied for six years by the Allies, mainly the United States. As a nation, Japan was (and still is) unique in the world in having experienced the horror of a nuclear attack. Yet the Japanese transition to nonviolence developed gradually. As a war-torn world began to realize the extent of the Holocaust and the immense number of Stalin's victims, the Japanese started to acknowledge their aggression toward other Asians in the Pacific and their own war crimes. This intense period was also one of enormous flux as leaders set up a new government and rewrote the 1890 Meiji Constitution. That constitution had been promulgated under Emperor Hirohito's grandfather, who was considered a deity (as was his son and grandson until after World War II, when the emperor's religious role was recast). In 1947 the Japanese Diet (parliament) debated a draft constitution for 114 days, made revisions and accepted the final version, which included Article 9, a controversial prohibition against Japan's maintaining an offensive military or using force internationally for any reason. In its entirety Article 9 reads:

> 1. Aspiring sincerely to an international peace based on justice and order, the Japanese people forever renounce war as a sovereign right of the nation and the threat or use of force as means of settling international disputes.

> 2. In order to accomplish the aim of the preceding paragraph, land, sea, and air forces, as well as other war potential, will never be maintained. The right of belligerency of the state will not be recognized.

Scholars have advanced several reasons to explain why Japan, acting in contrast to its highly militarized past, so readily agreed to limit its military. It is said that Japan envisioned itself becoming a neutral nation like Sweden or Switzerland and that by not having to rebuild its military, while under the protection of the United States, Japan could focus on rebuilding its economy.

Meanwhile, as the Japanese public embraced a new Constitution, a new government and a new understanding of their emperor, it also began to internalize the pacifist ethic that still characterizes a majority today, particularly regarding nuclear arms and proliferation.

During those same years the U.S.S.R. united its postwar land gains and pursued Communist world domination, emerging as the new threat to world peace. Japan's proximity to both Communist Russia and China was particularly advantageous to America's anti-Communist strategy. As early as the Eisenhower administration, the U.S. government had second thoughts about having urged institutionalized pacifism on Japan, which weakened it as an ally. On the other hand, some scholars argue that Japanese leaders saw Article 9 as a potential defense, shielding Japan from being caught between the two cold war superpowers.

In signing the 1951 Mutual Security Treaty and the 1954 Mutual Defense Assistance Agreement, the United States promised to protect Japan, and Japan allowed the United States to use its territory for permanent military bases. The latter agreement also permitted Japan to maintain a limited Self-Defense Force to protect its mainland.

Since the end of the cold war, three unlikely streams continued to run alongside one another in Japan. First, nonaggression and nuclear pacifism have become a part of Japanese culture and identity. The signs are various. Not only did Japan sign the Nuclear Non-Proliferation Treaty and refrain from building or trading in nuclear arms; but according to polls conducted over the last few decades, more than 70 percent of Japanese have consistently opposed nuclear weapons. As a nation Japan did not intervene during the Vietnam War, after a citizen campaign of protest, and rejected U.S. pressure to send members of the Japanese Self-Defense Force to support the United States during the first Persian Gulf war.

Second, Japan's S.D.F. has grown substantially in size and strength. Its navy, air force and army together employ 240,000 people (according to 2006 data). And Japan's $50 billion annual defense budget is the world's third largest after those of the United States and Russia, though China's (which is not publicly known) might be larger.

Third, the U.S. troops and weapons on Japanese soil have increased in number, size and power. Some 50,000 U.S. troops currently reside on more than 130 military installations, mostly on Okinawa—all at Japanese expense, the troop salaries excepted.

In addition to these three streams, Japan has breached its own self-defense policy on a number of occasions, beginning in Cambodia in 1992, when Japan sent some 2,000 "peacekeepers," including members of its military, to Cambodia under the auspices of the U.N. to monitor a ceasefire, train civilian police and engineer the repair of roads and bridges. Japan's role in world peacekeeping has grown since then.

By the time the Soviet Union split up in the early 1990s, Japan and the United States had become strong allies with social, cultural, political and economic ties. Japan's economy boomed, and Japan became one of the world's richest nations. The cold war era ended and another era began.

CHANGING ROLE ON THE WORLD STAGE

Enter China. Asia's sleeping giant has awakened. As the behemoth labors to develop its economy and shape its new international role, Japan is being forced to adjust its self-image, regional strategy and position in the world. North Korea's nuclear testing and posturing and Pakistan's interest in nuclear arms, heightened by its role in the wars in Afghanistan and Iraq, have scarcely gone unnoticed in Japan. Add to the picture a newly aggressive Russia, flush with oil profits, looming to the northwest over Japan's shoulder and it becomes apparent that Japan cannot remain unaffected or indifferent. A nuclear Asia is at hand. What does that prospect mean for Japan? This is a matter for significant public thought and conversation, which should be reflected in the kind of leaders Japan chooses to govern it.

But that is not all. Since the attacks of Sept. 11, 2001, the United States has become engulfed in a "war on terror" and is mired in the Middle East, its troops stretched thin. How secure is Japan now with the United States as its protector? Does Japan's protectorate position promote regional peace or work against it? The Bush administration has urged Japanese leaders to remove its constitutional restraint and take on more responsibility for regional defense. Given such increasing pressures, it is not surprising that two Japanese prime ministers, Junichiro Koizumi and after him Shinzo Abe, have pushed for a referendum to amend the Constitution, particularly the clause on international collective defense in Article 9. This seems to be in abeyance under the new prime minister, Yasuo Fukuda, who is thought to be more cautious in military matters. But the issues will not simply fade away.

The choice facing the Japanese is not a new one, since Japan has already leaned away from its Constitution. It has broken precedent (Archbishop Takami says it has violated its Constitution) by using military force beyond its borders. In 2001 the S.D.F. sank a North Korean spy ship; recently Japan has sent troops to Afghanistan and Iraq as part of the "coalition of the willing." Technically Japanese troops do not engage in combat there but provide logistical support. Japan is also aware that its Self-Defense Force is ill-equipped for offensive actions: its navy has no nuclear submarines or aircraft carriers and its three military branches lack both coordination and efficient communication. In 2006, the Diet introduced a bill to consolidate oversight of these operations and change the name of the ministry.

At Georgetown Archbishop Takami cited bilateral agreements of 2005 (the U.S.-Japan Alliance) and 2006 (the Roadmap for Realignment Implementation), by which, he said, "Japan has been made a major hub for American military operations all over the world, transforming the Japanese military forces into part of the globally deployed U.S. military forces." The archbishop questioned the legality of the process, intimating that it may require formal treaty revisions "through democratic procedures." He also said that Japan has committed itself "to full participation in ballistic missile defense, counterterrorism, search and destroy operations, intelligence, surveillance and reconnaissance operations, through response to attacks by weapons of mass destruction and joint use of bases and facilities in Japan with the Self-Defense Force to the U.S. use of seaport and airport facilities, roads, water spaces, airspaces, and frequency bands." The complete list is cumulatively more troubling. These agreements violate Japan's Constitution, yet they have been agreed to by the two governments, even as constitutional change is being discussed without strong support for change among Japanese voters.

Political leaders have also sidestepped Japan's popular no-nuclear policy. According to Archbishop Takami, 546 Tomahawk missiles are already in place on U.S. warships at Yokosuka, and the nuclear submarine George Washington will be deployed there next year. A citizens' movement against its deployment collected 500,000 signatures, and the city council passed a resolution opposing it in 2005; but "the mayor now defends the Yokosuka base as the forefront of the ballistic missile defense," the archbishop reported. He added that "Okinawa has the biggest arsenal in Asia that can store more than 50,000 tons of ammunition in 500 installations."

The Japanese people's post-World War II commitment to nonviolence and against nuclear weapons must be updated in light of such recent developments. And Japan's relationship to the United States needs to be publicly aired and assessed. The questions facing Japan are serious. Can Japan remain dependent upon the United States and willfully unable to protect itself, even as more large or unstable nations nearby acquire nuclear weapons? Is that prudent? Does Japan—apart from the promptings of the United States—wish to address the worldwide war on terror? If so, how? How can Japan strengthen and balance its relationships to China, North Korea, India and Pakistan, among others? If Japan amended its "peace constitution," shed its military dependency and became a major military power in the region, would that increase Japan's security and stability and the peace of Asia?

Japan could make a firm recommitment to peace and renegotiate its military agreements with the United States. Or Japan could amend its Constitution and existing treaties so that these reflect its current policy. Or Japan could take a whole new direction in terms of national goals and policies, take over its own military affairs and require the U.S. troops to leave.

The direction Japanese voters will prefer is difficult to predict. While there seems to be no current groundswell of support for a full militarization of Japan, support is growing on the margins. In an upper-house election in July, the people voted in a landslide election for members of the Democratic Party, the party in opposition to that of the prime minister (the Liberal Democratic Party). Commentators interpreted the vote as displeasure with Abe's domestic scandals and policy blunders, which later brought about his downfall.

Unwittingly, the voters have bought some time for those who oppose efforts to revise the pacifist Constitution. Opponents may well redouble their efforts to make a persuasive case for peace. Opponents include the Japanese Catholic Bishops Conference, which prefers to keep Article 9 as it is and to fortify the nation's commitment to nonviolence as a world witness to peace, and the current mayor of Nagasaki, Tomihisa Taue. In his remarks at Nagasaki's Peace Park, Mayor Taue warned against the perils of nuclear proliferation and proposed that Japan's three non-nuclear principles, which ban the possession, production and importation of nuclear armaments, be enacted into law. "The use of nuclear weapons can never be permitted or considered acceptable for any reason whatsoever," Taue said. What the Japanese people as a whole must decide is whether they, as victims of atomic weapons, will become potential perpetrators.

6

South Korea: The 38th Parallel and Beyond

Editor's Introduction

On July 27, 1953, the United Nations, China, and North Korea signed an armistice, effectively—though not technically—ending the three-year-old Korean War. By that time, the Cold War's first major military conflict had claimed the lives of some 4 million people, including 50,000 U.S. troops. When the ink dried and dust settled, things hadn't much changed on the Korean Peninsula. The communists controlled the North, an American-backed democratic regime ran the South, and a 2.5-mile "demilitarized zone" separated the two.

In the nearly 60 years since the armistice—a document South Korea refused to sign—American forces have stayed put, operating dozens of bases. Throughout the 1950s and '60s, troop levels hovered between 50,000 and 60,000. Such massive deployments made sense, given the possibility of renewed Korean hostilities and the peninsula's strategic location in Northeast Asia, a Cold War hotspot. Following the fall of the Soviet Union, the rationale for maintaining troops in South Korea became less clear. The West's major worry was no longer that North Korea would launch a Russian- or Chinese-backed invasion of the South, but rather that the increasingly isolated, destitute nation would develop and deploy nuclear weapons.

Experts believe North Korea has, indeed, joined the nuclear club, and even if ruling dictator Kim Jong-il lacks a long-range delivery system, some pundits argue that his defiant international posturing necessitates the United States maintaining its present troop level—roughly 28,500. Others maintain it's illogical to leave "conventional" U.S. forces on the Korean Peninsula, where they're prime targets for nuclear attack.

The pieces in this chapter provide an overview of the U.S.-South Korean alliance, examining how the military partnership has evolved over the years, as well as how it could continue to change in the future. In the first article, "USFK Seeks to Expand Role Outside Peninsula," Jung Sung-ki discusses the "strategic flexibility" now being sought by the U.S. Forces Korea (USFK). No longer content to simply stand guard against North Korea—a task South Korea can handle itself—the U.S. military is seeking to play a greater role in regional affairs. While some South Koreans fear the United States' shift in focus will create a "security vacuum" and invite attacks from the North, military officials insist they will remain committed to keeping Kim Jong-il in check.

In "Letting Go," the subsequent piece, Doug Bandow describes the United States' partnership with South Korea as "trapped in the past." He proposes signing a peace treaty with North Korea—a document that would replace the armistice and formally end the Korean War—and leaving the South to handle its own defense. While he urges continued cooperation with South Korea, he insists the country "should be dependent on Washington no more."

In "S. Korea Expands Modern Forces as It Seeks Greater Security Role," the following piece, the author details the size and scope of the South Korean military, highlighting its "120 warships, 490 fighter jets and 2,300 tanks," as well as its $20-billion 2009 defense budget. These figures speak to the country's ability to defend itself, perhaps proving Bandow's point.

A writer for the *Korea Times* considers how U.S. involvement in Asian affairs could affect South Korea's relations with its neighbors in the final article, "New US Command." "A U.S. military presence is seen as inevitable here," the author comments, "but this does not necessarily mean that the nation has to sacrifice its interests in return for security." The writer calls on South Korea to "play more on equal footing" with the Americans on foreign-policy matters.

USFK Seeks to Expand Role Outside Peninsula*

By Jung Sung-ki
Korea Times, February 24, 2010

After its decades-long stationary mission in South Korea, the U.S. Forces Korea (USFK) is taking steps toward expanding its missions to outside the Korean Peninsula, which U.S. defense officials do not consider an acting war zone anymore.

The USFK says the so-called strategic flexibility will not hurt its security commitment to South Korea against a possible North Korean invasion and instead help ensure its stable commitment with longer, family-accompanied tours by U.S. service members here.

Still, there are worries that such flexibility for out-of-area deployment of US troops will weaken the combined defense posture against North Korea.

A senior official at the Ministry of National Defense said last week that South Korean and U.S. defense authorities had opened talks over the issue formally.

"The two governments had already agreed on the issue of strategic flexibility in January 2006, so both sides are discussing how and when the scheme will be implemented," the official said on condition of anonymity. "We're trying to finalize an agreement by the year's end, hopefully before the Security Consultative Meeting (SCM) in October."

The official noted his ministry was focusing on getting proper U.S. bridging capability of intelligence-gathering, surveillance and reconnaissance to South Korea despite the U.S. flexible troop redeployment.

NO IMMEDIATE PLAN TO REDEPLOY TROOPS

The USFK says it has no immediate plan to redeploy troops from the peninsula but the issue will evolve in coming years. It said in a news release earlier this month that redeployment of troops could be possible in the late 2010s after close consultations with the Korean government.

There are currently about 28,500 U.S. troops serving in South Korea. Despite Washington's repeated promises there will be no further cuts to that level, concerns persist that some may be redeployed after Seoul takes back wartime operational control, or OPCON, of its troops from the U.S. on April 17, 2012.

The defense of South Korea "remains the core mission of U.S. forces in Korea and there will be no reduction of U.S. forces tied to wartime OPCON transition," the USFK said in the statement.

In 2006, South Korea agreed to the U.S. strategic flexibility plan aimed at changing the mission of American forces abroad from stationary ones defending host nations to rapid deployment troops that can be swiftly dispatched to other parts of the world where the United States faces conflict, based on mutual consensus.

The agreement, however, ignited concerns that it could weaken the deterrent capability against North Korea, whose nuclear and missile programs pose a grave threat to regional security.

Some are also worried that intervention by the USFK in other regional conflicts, such as the China-Taiwan sovereignty dispute, or the U.S. wars in Iraq and Afghanistan, could have the nation tangled in hostilities with other countries against its will.

"The strategic flexibility is part of the U.S. military's broader plan to realign its overseas forces, so that's not directly related to Seoul's exercise of independent wartime operational control in 2012," a senior researcher of the Korea Institute for Defense Analyses (KIDA) said on condition of anonymity. "But it's quite certain that as Seoul assumes more responsibility for national defense in coming years, the U.S. military will have more flexibility in moving its forces in and out of the peninsula."

"The thing is how the U.S. will compensate for the 'flow-out' capability," he added. "Personally, I don't believe there will be a significant security vacuum here due to the strategic flexibility scheme, given the U.S. military's overwhelming naval- and air-centric capabilities."

Another defense expert said the strategic flexibility of U.S. troops overseas is an unavoidable "trend."

He said, "The strategic flexibility is not a matter of conflict but a matter of consultation or coordination. It's time for us to think of what we can get from the U.S. strategic flexibility, not what we can lose from it."

Given that the agreed 21st strategic alliance partnership calls for boosting bilateral cooperation in global issues, we can't and shouldn't deny the strategic flexibility mechanism, said the expert.

"The Lee government should think of how it will get this message across to the public and prevent unnecessary controversy over this issue," he said.

In June, Presidents Lee Myung-bak and Barack Obama issued the Joint Vision for the ROK-US Alliance at the end of their summit in Washington, D.C. The plan calls for building a broader alliance in the realms of politics, economy, culture and other areas, in addition to the security arena.

'NO MORE COMBAT ZONE'

The U.S. Department of Defense approved a new USFK policy in December 2008 that allows about half of its 28,000 troops stationed in South Korea to have their families live with them.

The move reflects a major shift in the American perception toward South Korea, which was once considered too dangerous for families in the face of North Korea's military threats.

The extended tour length will contribute to further solidify the Korea-U.S. alliance by forging lifelong friendships at the family level, USFK officials said. It will also help improve training for service members and reduce stress on troops who have to leave their families behind, they said.

"Tour normalization signals a strong and visible commitment by the United States to the Republic of Korea, reaffirming our intent to remain here for the long term," USFK Commander Gen. Walter Sharp said in an interview last year.

"I will say that tour normalization will help establish a strong alliance relationship," he continued. "The principle institutions of the alliance today—the armistice, short tours and the contingency nature of the Combined Forces Command—all have crisis connotations."

The planned transition of operational control of Korean troops during wartime from the United States to South Korea in 2012 and the tour normalization initiative will move U.S. troops beyond this "crisis mentality," said the commander.

Under the new policy, troops serving in accompanied billets, including Seoul, Osan, Pyeongtaek, Daegu and Jinhae, will stay for three years, while those serving in locations just south of the heavily fortified border, designated Area I, such as Uijeongbu and Dongducheon, will stay for two years.

Unaccompanied tours for most troops will remain at one year, but some "key personnel" will serve two years of unaccompanied tours.

Letting Go[*]

By Doug Bandow
The American Spectator, January 25, 2010

South Korean defense minister Kim Tae-young wants his nation to initiate a pre-emptive assault if it appears that the North is preparing a nuclear attack. The Republic of Korea "should immediately launch a strike," said Kim.

Such a policy makes obvious sense. However, it leads to the question: if the ROK is strong enough to initiate war, why does the U.S. continue to defend the South?

The U.S.-South Korean mutual defense treaty dates back to 1953, after the Korean War ended in stalemate. Only American military support then preserved the ROK's independence in the face of the heavily militarized Democratic People's Republic of Korea, backed by China and the Soviet Union.

However, that world long ago disappeared. There is no more Soviet Union. Today's China would not support North Korean aggression. And South Korea vastly outmatches the decrepit DPRK on virtually every measure of national power. Pyongyang has a bigger military, but the South's quality counterbalances the North's quantity.

Moreover, Seoul is capable of doing far more. With an economy ranked in the world's top 15, South Korea has roughly 40 times the GDP of the North, strong high-tech industries, and ample international credit; the South also possesses twice the population of its northern antagonist. In short, Seoul can easily outmatch Pyongyang.

Why are nearly 30,000 U.S. troops still on station?

The DPRK recently proposed signing a peace treaty with the U.S. to replace the existing armistice agreement. Washington demurred, explaining that normal relations were impossible until Pyongyang abandoned its nuclear program. State Department spokesman P.J. Crowley stated: "We're not going to pay North Korea to come back to the six-party process."

But a peace treaty should not be seen as a reward for the North. Rather, it would simply formalize the end of hostilities 57 years late. Whether Washington should open diplomatic relations or end economic sanctions are different questions.

Agreeing to discuss terms of peace would offer two benefits. The first would be to place the U.S. and the DPRK, and perhaps also Seoul, in a simple negotiation where the outcome could benefit all sides. The issue is mostly symbolic—the North obviously would remain a danger even if it signed such a treaty. But eliminating today's formal state of war might advance talks with Pyongyang.

Admittedly, the odds of reaching an enforceable denuclearization agreement are slim. Nuclear weapons provide the North with numerous benefits. The best hope is pushing for a "grand bargain" backed by China. Even then the odds that the Kim regime, facing a leadership transition, would give up its most potent weapon are slim at best. But given the lack of good alternatives—military strikes could trigger a full-scale war while enhanced sanctions would require Beijing's consent—the diplomatic effort is worth pursuing, despite the scant chance of success.

The second benefit of such an agreement is more particular to the U.S. There's no reason, even during a formal state of war, for America to defend the South. The argument for a U.S. defense guarantee looks even weaker if the parties officially end today's state of hostilities.

Washington already is reducing its role. U.S. troop levels have fallen from 36,000 to 28,500 over the last decade. In 2012 the Pentagon will turn over wartime operational command (OPCON) of Korean forces to Seoul.

It's time to finish the process, pulling out the rest of America's troops and ending Washington's security guarantee. Despite efforts to refashion and "strengthen" the alliance, its raison d'être has disappeared.

The protection of the ROK always was vital to the ROK. With the Cold War over, South Korea's security no longer is of great concern to Washington. There is no international communist menace behind a potential North Korean attack.

Moreover, threats against the South are fading: a decrepit North increasingly is incapable of winning a war. Neither Japan nor China has any interest in conflict; even a more aggressive and powerful Beijing is not likely to resort to arms against the ROK. And Seoul is capable of creating a potent defense.

America's security priorities are broader—fighting terrorism and confronting potential hostile global hegemonic powers. But the first doesn't require large military forces and the second doesn't currently exist. Nor will bilateral military cooperation over such issues be easy.

South Korea is not threatened by Islamic terrorism and Seoul has little interest in the difficult task of creating a friendly government in Kabul. The South plans to dispatch 350 soldiers to Afghanistan, but for the purpose of buttressing U.S. support for continuing the alliance.

The plan is controversial in South Korea and of little practical value to America. In fact, it would be better if the ROK devoted its full resources to raising, equipping, and training adequate forces for action on the Korean peninsula. Seoul can do far more to defend itself than remake Afghanistan. The latter mission is a diversion.

Although willing to make a gesture regarding Afghanistan, the South is unlikely to cooperate with the U.S. against China, a Washington priority. South Korea doesn't want to become a permanent enemy of the colossus next door in service of America's broader geopolitical interests. It is one thing for Seoul to seek U.S. aid in the unlikely event of attempted Chinese coercion of the South; it is quite another for South Korea to join Washington in a war to defend, say, Taiwan.

There are lots of other suggested areas of cooperation, such as international development and UN peacekeeping, but none of these grow out of today's bilateral relationship—and especially America's essentially unilateral security guarantee. Whatever the future of ROK-U.S. relations, there is no need for America to defend the South.

That doesn't mean the two governments should not cooperate: both have an interest in a stable and prosperous East Asia. But their cooperation should be issue-by-issue, whether informal and bilateral or formal and multilateral.

U.S. policy towards South Korea remains trapped in the past. Adm. Timothy Keating, America's commander in the Asia-Pacific, recently announced: "We are prepared to execute a wide range of options in concert with allies in South Korea" against North Korea, if necessary. But shouldn't the ROK execute those options? Gen. Walter Sharp, U.S. commander in the South, said that allied forces are ready for "anything North Korea can throw at us." Shouldn't South Korea be ready?

There also has been discussion of an American military role in occupying the North should the Kim regime collapse, and even in combating any resulting insurgency. Why should the U.S. intervene in an area of primary concern to the increasingly capable ROK?

That coping with a North Korean collapse might be expensive and burdensome is true, but it is time for America's prosperous and populous friends and allies to begin coping with their problems. Washington remains very busy, facing an escalating and lengthy war in Afghanistan. Moreover, with annual deficits of $1 trillion projected for the next decade, Washington is out of money. The U.S. should stop underwriting the security costs of other nations.

A South Korean policy of pre-emptive war makes sense—for South Korea. But Seoul should accept the full costs of its own strategy. The ROK should be dependent on Washington no more.

S. Korea Expands Modern Forces as It Seeks
Greater Security Role[*]

Asia Pulse, April 24, 2009

After the three-year Korean War that ended in 1953 with a truce, South Korea was left with nearly non-existent naval and air forces and a bruised army that depended heavily on U.S. support.

But buoyed by rapid economic growth over the following decades, the country now operates a modern 655,000-strong force backed by 120 warships, 490 fighter jets and 2,300 tanks. As the world's 13th-largest economy, it will spend over $20US billion on defense this year alone.

"We can't help feeling emotionally overwhelmed when we think of how far we've come," Vice Admiral Park Chung-hwa recently said while aboard the 4,500-ton Wang Geon destroyer in Busan.

The destroyer, docked at the Naval Force Operations Command (NFOC) in the southeastern city, is one of South Korea's latest warships, built with guided missiles and radars that can knock out entire communication systems in surrounding regions.

Showing a giant screen inside the NFOC that tracks all vessels operating near the Yellow Sea border—the scene of bloody battles between the Koreas in 1999 and 2002—Park said his navy is aiming higher than what most would like to think.

"Our immediate goal is to deter North Korean aggression, but we need to expand our naval forces if we are to contribute more to global and regional security," he said.

South Korea recently sent a destroyer to Somali waters, where it joined a U.S.-led anti-piracy campaign. The crew of 300 is part of hundreds of South Korean forces serving worldwide as part of either multinational or U.N. peacekeeping operations, including in Lebanon.

"We could not have thought of such an operation had we not tried to expand our navy," Park said.

* Courtesy of Asia Pulse and AAP (Australian Associated Press).

South Korea currently operates a single Aegis-guided destroyer, Sejong the Great, but plans to build more as the country is backed by one of the most advanced shipbuilding industries in the world.

Even as the role South Korea plays expands, its focus remains on maintaining effective deterrence against North Korea, Captain Song Gi-seong said.

"North Korea still poses the single greatest threat to us," he said, speaking inside the SS Jung Ji, the latest submarine built by South Korea.

"North Korea is also developing and producing submarines on its own," he said, adding the North is believed to have constructed a number of underwater bunkers to anchor its submarines, making it difficult for enemies to track their activities.

According to the latest South Korean defense white book, North Korea has seven times more submarines than its southern neighbor.

But many of them are outdated, analysts say, and numbers do not tell everything when it comes to comparing the conventional forces of the two countries.

"North Korea has failed to catch up with the latest trends in defense technology and refine its armory because of its isolation and its deteriorating economy," Baek Seung-joo, a researcher at the state-funded Korea Institute for Defense Analyses in Seoul, said.

"That is one of the reasons the North is holding on to its nuclear ambitions," he said.

North Korea is believed to have enough plutonium to make up to six nuclear bombs, while the U.S. has guaranteed South Korea deterrence under a nuclear umbrella.

About 28,500 U.S. forces continue to serve in South Korea, forming the backbone of the Seoul-Washington military alliance and monitoring the movement of frontline North Korean troops.

But the U.S. is increasingly relinquishing its role on the Korean Peninsula to South Korea as it relocates most of its forces further south of the border and prepares to return wartime operational control of South Korean troops to Seoul in 2012.

South Korea gave control to the U.S. at the onset of the Korean War. The peacetime command was returned in 1994.

Ties between the allies will likely remain strong even after the full transfer, partly because South Korea still needs to learn much from the U.S. in air force training, Brigadier General Kwon Oh-bong of 17th Fighter Group said at an airbase in the city of Cheongju, 120 km south of Seoul.

The airbase, home to a range of fighters including F-4s and F-16s, serves as a key base for launching retaliatory strikes against North Korea because it is only 150 km from the border, military experts say.

Kwon declined to elaborate on the mission of his unit, but expressed confidence that his country's Air Force has surpassed that of North Korea in terms of training and tactical capability.

"We fly hundreds of training sorties each day, whereas North Korea struggles to secure enough fuel to lift their airplanes," he said.

Colonel Choi Hyun-kook, South Korea's top pilot trainer, said North Korea has secured advanced fighter jets, but lacks ground radars and other facilities to support them.

"Modern warfare isn't just about the capabilities of each fighter," he said, speaking in front of a satellite-guided pilot training system that tracks the movement of fighter jets practicing maneuvers as either friendly or enemy aircraft.

Choi added his Air Force has secured data on the flight characteristics of over a dozen missiles used by North Korean aircraft, incorporating it into its training system.

"We continue to upgrade our system so our pilots can be as sufficiently prepared as U.S. pilots, especially during combined exercises," he said.

Baek, the analyst, said the expanding strength of the South Korean military is a result not only of the rivalry on the Korean Peninsula but also of the end of the Cold War on a global scale.

"Each country is now free to pursue military strength on par with its economic standing, unencumbered by restrictions that had been imposed by its superpower ally," he said.

"South Korea is no different, and it is more confident than ever as it expands armed forces that are backed by its economic spending and the military alliance with the U.S."

New US Command[*]

Korea Needs to Maximize Benefits, Minimize Burdens

Korea Times, November 8, 2008

The U.S. Forces Korea (USFK) on Friday disclosed a plan to keep the Eighth U.S. Army (EUSA) in South Korea even after it hands over wartime operational control to Seoul in 2012. There is no question that the American military highly recognizes the strategic importance of the Korean Peninsula. In this sense, the continued presence of EUSA in the country will help ease some worries among South Koreans about a potential security vacuum that may be created by a possible relocation to Hawaii.

Instead of the relocation plan, the USFK is to create a new theater command—Korea Command (KORCOM)—around June next year. The envisioned command is seen as part of U.S. efforts to restructure its forces stationed in South Korea in line with its global military strategy. KORCOM is expected to serve as a frontline military foothold for the U.S. in Northeast Asia under its global policy of "strategic flexibility." Thus, the role of the USFK is likely to shift from its exclusive defense of South Korea to redeployment of forces to other disputed regions around the world.

Considering South Korea's geopolitical situation, the continued stationing of EUSA and the establishment of KORCOM is a boon to the nation's security and defense. Especially since the North Korean nuclear crisis has yet to be resolved, some military experts as well as ordinary citizens cannot shake off concerns about escalating threats from the Kim Jong-il regime.

Under a 2007 agreement between Seoul and Washington, the South Korean military is scheduled to take over wartime operational control of its armed forces from the U.S. on April 17, 2012. Both sides also agreed to disband the Korea-U.S. Combined Forces Command (CFC) and run separate theater commands. The USFK said the EUSA transformation, including its

---

planned move to Pyeongtaek, south of Seoul, confirms the U.S. commitment to a strong bilateral alliance and the defense of the Korean people.

In fact, EUSA has played a pivotal role to help defend South Korea, along with the United Nations Command (UNC) during the 1950-53 Korean War. But it is also true that the army's function has been waning since the 1978 establishment of the CFC, which takes charge of wartime operations on the peninsula. We must keep in mind that the U.S. has been actively seeking to maximize the effective operations of its overseas troops.

Some critics point out that Washington's strategic focus is placed more on its national interests than on those of its allies. They also note that the transformation of the U.S. military in Korea should be understood in a boarder context as Japan under the new leadership of Prime Minister Yukio Hatoyama may review its military alliance with America. The creation of KORCOM may negatively affect South Korea's ties with China and Russia, whose strategic interests could clash with those of the U.S. in Northeast Asia.

A U.S. military presence is seen as inevitable here. But this does not necessarily mean that the nation has to sacrifice its interests in return for security. Therefore, it is urgent for policymakers to make efforts to minimize the adverse effects and burdens of the changing USFK structure on the Korean side. What is also important is that as the host country, South Korea needs to play more on an equal footing with the U.S. in order to cement the partnership between the two countries.

Bibliography

Books

Bacevich, Andrew. *The Limits of Power: The End of American Exceptionalism*. New York: Metropolitan Books, 2008.

Bacevich, Andrew. *The New American Militarism: How Americans Are Seduced by War*. New York: Oxford University Press, 2005.

Baker, Anni P. *American Soldiers Overseas: The Global Military Presence*. Westport, CT: Praeger Publishers, 2004.

Bandow, Doug. *The Korean Conundrum: America's Troubled Relations with North and South Korea*. New York: Palgrave Macmillan, 2004.

Calder, Kent E. *Embattled Garrisons: Comparative Base Politics and American Globalism*. Princeton, N.J.: Princeton University Press, 2007.

Carkoglu, Ali and Ersin Kalaycioglu. *The Rising Tide of Conservatism in Turkey*. New York: Palgrave Macmillan, 2009.

Cooley, Alexander. *Base Politics: Democratic Change and the U.S. Military Overseas*. Ithaca, NY: Cornell University Press, 2008.

Ferguson, Niall. *Colossus: The Price of America's Empire*. New York: The Penguin Press, 2004.

Gillem, Mark L. *America Town: Building the Outposts of Empire*. Minneapolis, MN: University of Minnesota Press, 2007.

Inoue, Masamichi, S. *Okinawa and the U.S. Military: Identity Making in the Age of Globalization*. New York: Columbia University Press, 2007.

Johnson, Chalmers. *Blowback: The Costs and Consequences of American Empire, Second Edition*. New York: Henry Holt and Company, LLC, 2000.

Johnson, Chalmers. *The Sorrows of Empire*. New York: Metropolitan Books, 2004.

Jones, Seth G. *In the Graveyard of Empires: America's War in Afghanistan*. New York: W. W. Norton & Company, 2010.

Kagan, Kimberly. *The Surge: A Military History*. New York: Encounter Books, 2009.

King, Erika G. and Robert A. Wells. *Framing the Iraq War Endgame: War's Denouement in an Age of Terror*. New York: Palgrave Macmillan, 2009.

Layne, Christopher and Bradley A. Thayer. *American Empire: A Debate*. New York: Routledge, 2007.

Lee, Chae-Jin. *A Troubled Peace: U.S. Policy and the Two Koreas*. Baltimore: The Johns Hopkins University Press, 2006.

Loyn, David. *In Afghanistan: 200 Years of British, Russian, and American Occupation*. New York: Palgrave Macmillan, 2009.

Lutz, Catherine. *The Bases of Empire: The Global Struggle against U.S. Military Posts*. New York: New York University Press, 2009.

Perkins, John. *The Secret History of the American Empire: Economic Hit Men, Jackals, and the Truth about Global Corruption*. New York: Plume, 2008.

Riedel, Bruce. *The Search for Al Qaeda: Its Leadership, Ideology, and Future*, Revised edition. Washington, D.C.: The Brookings Institution, 2008.

Robinson, Linda. *Tell Me How This Ends: General David Petraeus and the Search for a Way Out of Iraq*. New York: Public Affairs, 2008.

Vine, David. *Island of Shame: The Secret History of the U.S. Military Base on Diego Garcia*. Princeton, N.J.: Princeton University Press, 2009.

West, Bing. *The Strongest Tribe: War, Politics, and the Endgame in Iraq*. New York: Random House, 2009.

Westad, Odd Arne. *The Global Cold War: Third World Interventions and the Making of Our Times*. New York: Cambridge University Press, 2005.

Zakaria, Fareed. *The Post-American World*. New York: W. W. Norton & Company, Inc., 2008.

Web Sites

Readers seeking additional information on the American military presence overseas and related topics may wish to consult the following Web sites, all of which were operational as of this writing.

North Atlantic Treaty Organization

www.nato.intl/

Established April 4, 1949, NATO aims to "safeguard the freedom and security of its member countries by political and military means." The international organization comprises 28 member nations, all located in North America and Europe, as well as a number of partner countries, including Russia, once the focus of NATO's containment strategies. The NATO Web site features archived speeches and news articles, as well as "NATO A-Z" section, which outlines the agency's various policies and initiatives.

United States Department of Defense

www.defense.gov

Covering all five branches of the U.S. military, this Web site is loaded with news updates, blog posts, speech transcripts, budgets, press releases, official reports, photos, bios of high-ranking personnel, and other useful information. The site also lists job openings and explains how one goes about enlisting in the armed services.

NO BASES: International Network for the Abolition of Foreign Military Bases

www.nobases.org

Formed in 2004, the International Network for the Abolition of Foreign Military Bases is committed to abolishing foreign military bases—installations maintained by the United States, primarily, but also other Western powers—and preventing the creation of new ones. The group supports local base-closure movements, and its Web site contains information on grassroots campaigns, links to relevant sites and news stories, and maps illustrating the prevalence of U.S. military bases around the world.

Additional Periodical Articles with Abstracts

More information about the U.S. military presence abroad can be found in the following articles. Readers interested in additional articles may consult the *Readers' Guide to Periodical Literature* and other H.W. Wilson publications.

Time For an Amicable Divorce with South Korea. Daniel Kennelly. *The American Enterprise* v. 16 pp36–38 July/August 2005.

In this article, part of a special section on relations between the U.S. and North Korea, Kennelly calls the current alliance with South Korea a diplomatic straitjacket that prevents the U.S. from acting decisively against North Korea. The nuclear-enabled North Korean regime poses serious dangers, risks proliferation to terrorists, and presents a likelihood of long-running threats and instability, Kennelly writes. As South Korea refuses to give consent to any military move, he adds, the U.S. must break the alliance so that it can have the choice of using force to eliminate North Korea's nuclear program.

The Ultimate Test Case. *American Prospect* v. 21 pp21–25 March 2010.

President Barack Obama's failure to reorient U.S. military goals within Afghanistan has serious ramifications for his proposed foreign-policy reforms, the author of this piece suggests. Obama has remained committed to a military solution to the problem of insurgency within Afghanistan, pledging to deploy 30,000 additional troops to the conflict zone. Nonetheless, many insurgents in the region are not ideological opponents of the U.S., the writer states, adding that Obama's commitment to a military defeat of al-Qaeda in Afghanistan and Pakistan could play into that organization's stated goal of drawing the U.S. into an intractable war. Success in Afghanistan, the author insists, could bring further credibility to Obama's other, more controversial foreign-policy goals, but using the military to fight terrorism in Afghanistan risks hindering the transformation of civilian agencies and prevents the president from allocating resources to other projects.

Japan and South Korea: Can These Two Nations Work Together? Kevin J. Cooney and Alex Scarbrough. *Asian Affairs* v. 34 p173–92 Fall 2008.

South Korea is Japan's most logical ally in East Asia, the authors contend, explaining that both nations share the same primary military benefactor, the United States. Their geographic proximity makes them natural allies in offsetting China's growing power and unknown intentions, the authors insist. In spite of the many reasons to ally, relations remain strained, primarily because of Japan's historical occupation of Korea. In this article, the authors examine the political issues that must be resolved for Japan and South Korea to work together and the potential for such reconciliation in light of South Korea's on-again/off-again drift away from the United States and Japan's open embrace of U.S. protection and occasional political distancing.

Unraveling the Afghanistan-Pakistan Riddle. Lawrence Ziring. *Asian Affairs* v. 36 pp59–77 Summer 2009.

U.S. President Barack Obama made a campaign promise to the nation that, if elected, he would withdraw combat forces from Iraq and shift the focus of U.S. strategy from the Middle East to the border of Afghanistan and Pakistan, where a renascent and spreading Taliban movement harbors al Qaeda leaders and foot soldiers and threatens to reverse the forces of change in Afghanistan. Obama's declared intention to increase the number of U.S. troops in Afghanistan appears not only to have the general approval of his military advisers, but also to have won over many of the foreign and national security analysts both within and outside the administration. The author examines the wisdom of this policy now, before a thorough debate has occurred and before several significant issues have been addressed. Reprinted by permission of the publisher.

Wipeout. Jeanette Lee. *Atlantic Monthly* v. 304 pp24, 26 November 2009.

The U.S. military is going ahead with a $15 billion expansion of its facilities on Guam that promises to transform this tiny American territory. The most talked-about aspect of the enlargement process is the pending arrival from Okinawa, Japan, of 8,000 U.S. Marines, their families, and an accompanying civilian workforce, which will boost Guam's population by 15 to 30 percent by 2014. Although Guam's politicians, academics, indigenous activists, and some business owners are concerned about overcrowding and a potential lack of respect for the island and its inhabitants, many of them are maneuvering for as much federal money as possible.

Tax Dollars at Work. *The Christian Century* v. 124 p5 September 18, 2007.

The Department of Defense is very secretive about U.S. military bases located outside the United States, the author of this article writes. According to Chalmers Johnson's *Nemesis*, the United States officially has 737 military bases located in 132 of the 190 nations belonging to the UN. The official count does not include bases in Israel, Afghanistan, Iraq, and a number of other Middle Eastern nations, however. Johnson believes that the total number of foreign bases is over 1,000 and that even the Pentagon does not know exactly how many there are. The presence of U.S. military bases prompts resentment in many of the host nations, the author writes, adding that the conditions negotiated for the establishment of the bases are frequently not in the best interests of the host nations, and the long-term presence of war material can have devastating consequences for the local environment.

Into Africa. James J. Hentz. *Hoover Digest* pp114–20 Fall 2008.

A new military command is taking a broad, sophisticated view of the U.S. role in Africa, but the job will be a tough one, Hentz writes. A noble experiment in national security, the U.S. Africa Command (AFRICOM) is an ambitious reconfiguring of the military's role not just in Africa, but also in the world at large, the author insists. The new separate command for the neglected continent is aimed at moving beyond cold war arrangements, which saw Africa split among three U.S. military commands, and to address both new and lingering geopolitical problems. Africa Command was formed in February 2007 and started initial operations in October of that year. It is set to assume responsibility for all military relationships, programs, and activities in Africa in fall 2008 under its first commander, U.S. Army General William E. "Kip" Ward. To be successful, Hentz writes, AFRICOM must break free of four bad habits of the U.S. government, each of which tends to bolster the others.

American Power: Past Is Prologue. Thomas H. Henriksen. *Hoover Digest* pp82–90 Winter 2009.

The writer reviews U.S. foreign policy since the fall of the Berlin Wall in 1989. Reflecting on the lessons of the two decades since the fall of the Berlin Wall, he contends that President Barack Obama's new administration must retain military power as an option to counter terrorism and control nuclear-ambitious states such as Iran. Even so, Henriksen cautions that military power alone will be inadequate against terrorism and will neither guarantee U.S. security nor advance democratic values. America's multiyear conflicts in Afghanistan and Iraq may represent the end of an age of interventions and the start of an era of nonintervention, but it is more likely that the United States will become more reluctant to intervene overseas and will do so only with allies or with UN approval, the author insists. Past trends suggest that the U.S. government must do better at planning the outcomes of interventions, coordinating ends and means, and consolidating military triumphs with civic stability, Henriksen writes, adding that America's unipolar moment, despite its struggles in Iraq, is not over.

Mission Creep. Michael Mechanic. *Mother Jones* v. 33 pp66–7 September/October 2008.

Although the Bush administration announced it was slashing the number of U.S. military bases around the world, Mechanic writes, the move was not tantamount to a drawdown. The military, he reports, is actually expanding toward potential conflict zones, establishing bare-bones facilities in such countries as Romania, Bulgaria, and Kyrgyzstan. In Africa and elsewhere, it is negotiating access to "lily pads," or troop staging areas, and securing rights to stockpile provisions for later use. Despite the cost—an independent panel has estimated the realignment at $20 billion, five times the Pentagon's own estimate—the new facilities are largely missing from the government's public accounting. A map illustrates America's global military footprint.

Imperial Reach: The Pentagon's New Basing Strategy. Michael T. Klare. *The Nation* v. 280 pp13–14+ April 25, 2005.

As the Defense Department starts to look beyond the conflict in Iraq, a top priority will be to undertake a systematic realignment of U.S. forces and bases overseas. This huge project will lead to a substantial reduction in the American presence in Germany and South Korea and the establishment of new facilities in Eastern Europe, the Caspian Sea basin, Southeast Asia, and Africa. Such actions are generally justified in terms of military effectiveness, by removing obsolete cold war facilities and making it easier to move American soldiers to likely scenes of conflict, but this planning is underpinned by a new approach to combat and a revised calculus of the United States' geopolitical interests.

DMZ: Korea's Dangerous Divide. Tom O'Neil. *National Geographic* v. 204 pp2–27 July 2003.

Fifty years after the Korean War ended in an uneasy truce, two of the world's deadliest armies face each other across the Demilitarized Zone (DMZ). All along the

148-mile truce line that divides the Korean peninsula, hundreds of thousands of well trained soldiers from two of the world's biggest armies, as well as over 50 percent of the 37,000 American troops stationed in South Korea, stand ready to fight, trained by their commanders to loathe their ideological opposites and never allow their defense to slip. The conflict originated at the end of World War II, when the peninsula was split at the 38th parallel by the Soviet Union and America as the Allies drove Japan out of Korea. By 1953, nearly 900,000 troops had been killed, and over 2 million civilians had been killed or wounded, as the South Korean military, joined by UN troops, battled the forces of North Korea and China to a standstill. The writer discusses the instability of the DMZ and the potential for further conflict.

Seoul Searching: Ending the U.S.-Korean Alliance. Doug Bandow. *National Interest* pp111–16 Fall 2005.

The U.S. military alliance with South Korea is a relic from the Cold War that costs far more than it is worth, Bandow writes. The current relationship not only absorbs valuable military resources, the author insists, but keeps the Korean people in a dependent relationship that offends their nationhood and puts their destiny under the control of another country. The U.S. Cold War security concern over South Korea no longer exists, he adds, and even if it did, the alliance and U.S. troops are no longer necessary as the South has dramatically outstripped North Korea on virtually every measure of national power and can stand on its own.

The Yanks Are Leaving, and a Nation Can Rebuild Itself. Ewan Jones. *New Statesman* v. 134 pp32–33 January 10, 2005.

In this piece, published in early 2005, Jones argues that the future of the American GIs—long a visible, and hated, presence in South Korea—is uncertain. The expatriates face the prospect of displacement, partly because the excuse for America's continued military presence—to safeguard South Korea from the partitioned North—is beginning to lose plausibility; and partly because their services are required in Iraq, Jones writes. South Koreans' feelings about the departure of their unwelcome guests are complex; the U.S. played a large part in rebuilding the country after the 1950–53 Korean war, but resentment is growing, particularly over the perception of South Korea as a client state supporting U.S. global strategic aims. Jones contends the redeployment of the GIs may at least give South Korea an opportunity to define itself as an independent nation and address its own past.

Close to the Border. Martin Fletcher. *New Statesman* v. 136 p17 October 17, 2009.

In the fall of 2009, speculation was mounting concerning Turkey's plans to send troops into northern Iraq. Prime Minister Recep Tayyip Erdogan spoke of military operations against the separatist Kurdistan Workers' Party (PKK) bases there as though they were inevitable, Fletcher writes, noting that repeated requests to the Iraqi and U.S. governments to deal with the problem had been unsuccessful. Fletcher writes that Erdogan's comments were intended to reassure Turks that something would be done about the PKK attacks on Turkey and to goad the U.S. and Iraq into taking action themselves.

War Is Peace, Ignorance Is Strength. John Pilger. *New Statesman* v. 138 p22 October 19, 2009.

On July 15, 2009, the U.S. completed a deal with Colombia that gives the U.S. another seven huge military bases. According to the Associated Press, the objective is to provide the U.S. with a regional hub for military operations. What it means in reality, Pilger writes, is that Obama wants to roll back the independence that Bolivia, Venezuela, Ecuador, and Paraguay have achieved against the odds: Colombian paramilitaries have already infiltrated Venezuela with the aim of toppling the democratic government of Hugo Chávez. Obama may appeal to liberal sensibilities, Pilger insists, but his foreign policy suggests his approach to government is something different entirely.

U.S. Bases and Democratization in Central Asia. Alexander Cooley. *Orbis* v. 52 pp65–90 Winter 2008.

Under the Pentagon's current Global Defense Posture Review (GDPR), the United States is reducing its forces in several major Cold War base hosts and establishing a global network of smaller, more flexible facilities in new areas such as Central Asia, the Black Sea and Africa. Drawing upon recent evidence from the Central Asian base hosts of Kyrgyzstan and Uzbekistan, Cooley cautions that these new U.S. overseas bases, despite their lighter footprint and regardless of the prevailing security situation, risk becoming enmeshed in the local struggles and political agendas of elites within these hosts. Periods of turbulent democratic transition and regime instability may encourage host country politicians to challenge the legitimacy and terms of the U.S. basing presence for their own political purposes. These are important lessons for U.S. planners who are simultaneously promoting democratization while they negotiate basing and military access agreements in these same politically volatile hosts. Reprinted by permission of the publisher.

John Dear on the Audacity of Peace. John Dear. *Tikkun* v. 24 p46 January/February 2009.

In an open letter to newly elected U.S. president Barack Obama, Jesuit priest John Dear asks Obama to have the audacity to pursue peace. Among other things, he urges Obama to end the war in Iraq, dismantle nuclear weapons, close military bases, sign disarmament treaties with other nations, deploy the billions of dollars spent on war to rebuild the American economy and feed the world's starving masses, and start funding and institutionalizing nonviolent ways of resolving global conflicts.

Move 'Em Out. Julian E. Barnes. *U.S. News & World Report* v. 137 pp16–18+ August 30, 2004.

The outcome of the debate over the future of the American military will probably have a profound effect on how America projects its power in a quickly changing world, Barnes writes. The era of the large-scale, permanent American presence in Asia and Europe could be approaching its end, the author speculates, discussing President Bush's plan to pull back 70,000 of the 278,000 troops stationed in Germany, South Korea, and other overseas bases. Under this plan, the units were to return to America over ten years and then begin a rotation of short stints in places closer to the world's trouble spots. Generally, the Bush administration wanted a leaner and quicker military. Democrats believed that the plan would further alienate allies and give comfort to adversaries such as North Korea.

The Expeditionary Imperative. John A. Nagl. *The Wilson Quarterly* v. 33 pp5–58 Winter 2009.

In modern warfare, ideas and economic development are as important as heavy artillery, a lesson that the United States is only now learning. The U.S. response to the attacks of September 11, 2001, has focused disproportionately on military means, which have been unable to influence the underlying dynamics of a new and most serious kind of war—against a global insurgency. More than seven years into a global counterinsurgency campaign, America lacks many of the nonmilitary capabilities needed to secure, help, and reconstruct societies afflicted by insurgency and terrorism. Winning in today's conflicts calls for more than a few additional resources; it requires an expanded and better-coordinated expeditionary advisory initiative involving all agencies of the executive branch. It must also include a re-created U.S. Information Agency to present the U.S. case in the worldwide war of ideas.

The Human Element: When Gadgetry Becomes Strategy. H. R. McMaster. *World Affairs* v. 171 pp31–43 Winter 2009.

A fixation on U.S. technological superiority and an associated neglect of the human, psychological, and political dimensions of war are responsible for many of the errors of U.S. campaigns in Iraq and Afghanistan, McMaster writes. Although the Iraq and Afghanistan Wars differ significantly from the Vietnam War, he adds, some of the failed strategies of the latter have been applied to the current conflicts. Many of the military strategists involved in planning the Vietnam War made assumptions about the probable responses of their enemies to attack, erroneously basing these on theories of rational action. Similarly, the strategists of the current wars underestimated the reaction of the occupied populations, McMaster posits, expecting them to swiftly submit to U.S. technological prowess. The complexity, the author concludes, of all three situations—with their political, tribal, and emotional aspects—frustrates all attempts to predict the results of discrete military actions, however technologically empowered.

Cruel Realities: The American Conquest of Guam. Stephen Kinzer. *World Policy Journal* v. 23 p100–04 Summer 2006.

By taking the Pacific island of Guam from the Spanish in 1898, the U.S. secured an important strategic base from which to project commercial and military power, but U.S. rule has brought mixed results to the island itself, Kinzer writes. Guam remains a colonial ward of the U.S. Navy, and it is no exemplar of either democracy or native rights, Kinzer insists. Although some military governors worked some good for the island's development, the author adds, political rights were denied for over fifty years. Today, the author adds, an undercurrent of resentment exists below the surface of Guam's peaceful life: For some people on the island, economic and political progress does not make up for the lack of self-government and the loss of cultural identity.

The Emperor's New Clothes: Can Japan Live Without the Bomb? Masaru Tamamoto. *World Policy Journal* v. 26 pp 63–70 Fall 2009.

As U.S. president Barack Obama pursues a policy of nuclear decommissioning, Japan is becoming increasingly fearful that it will lose its protection under the U.S. "nuclear umbrella." Engaged in territorial disputes with all of its neighbors except North Korea, Japan is also worried that a bilateral non-aggression pact between the U.S. and North Korea would leave it exposed to conventional, chemical, or biological attack from the latter. The possibility of accruing its own nuclear arsenal is hampered by Japan's wish to avoid a de facto arms race with China and by pacifist public opinion, which has hailed Obama's decommissioning plans. The U.S. should instead encourage substantive discussions between China, Japan, and other northeast Asian countries, Tamamoto writes, in an attempt to enable them to further interlink their economies and move toward a viable nuclear decommissioning agreement.

Index

About the Editor

Writer, editor, and amateur military strategist—hence those green plastic army men he plays with on weekends—KENNETH PARTRIDGE has been with the H.W. Wilson Company since 2007. He spent a year writing for the company's *Current Biography* publication before joining the General Reference department, where he's edited four volumes of The Reference Shelf. Partridge, a Connecticut native and Boston University graduate, is also a freelance journalist, and he's written about rock and pop music for the *Hartford Courant*, *The Village Voice*, *USA Today*, and AOL Music, among other publications. He lives with his wife in Brooklyn, New York.